DEAR OPRAH

DEAR OPRAH

Alireza Ansari

RED FINCH PRODUCTIONS
San Rafael

Cover design by Laila Parsi.

ISBN: 978-1-940121-04-8

Red Finch Productions
Published by Urtext Media LLC
San Rafael, CA 94901
www.urtext.us

Printed in the United States of America

PROLOGUE

Most of us struggle with emotions caused by losses in our lives: jobs, loved ones, money, etc. But what we do have in our lives far outweighs what we have lost. There are billions of things and aspects to each of our lives that are positive, yet we are sad and suffer over losses without appreciating the good things we have.

The message I want to bring with this story is that we have only lost what we expected to have.

Maybe this expectation is wrong. Maybe we were not supposed to have the things we have lost in the first place.

Charlie Chaplin, the father of modern cinema, brought a similar message to his audience over a hundred years ago. But it didn't always work. Once when he was asked about his work he said that he had tried to show everything about life—both tragedy and comedy—but people only laughed. I believe Charlie Chaplin had two big obstacles in his time. First, people only thought of cinema as entertainment in those days and were not ready for the broad range of potential in movies. Second, because of technological limitations there was no dialog in most of his films, so often his messages were comprehended in a limited way.

I feel a personal affinity with Charlie Chaplin and often see the world through his eyes. In this book I would like to present how I see my life, which has gone through profound and challenging changes, through Charlie Chaplin's eyes. But not being a great artist like him I might be more successful in my task using language. I hope to use my story as a way to expand on what he was trying to say to us.

I would like to do this in honor of my hero, the great Charles Chaplin.

This is the story of an educated man with a prestigious career who left everything behind in his home country of Iran in search of a better future for his seven-year-old autistic son in America. Based on his expectations of life, the man was sure he would be a success. He felt certain of success because he had life experience and did not believe in insurmountable boundaries between people. He did not see national, religious or racial differences in the new country as obstacles. The only obstacle he saw for his family was language and he thought he knew English well enough. For example, he knew "water" is spelled w-a-t-e-r and even a longer word like "blackboard" is spelled b-l-a-c-k-b-o-a-r-d.

It was in this man's character to believe that whenever life presents you with a problem you must first laugh at it instead of crying over it, then find the key to solving it. Very simple— and this was his expectation.

Shortly after arrival in the U.S. and the start of his new life, he found things that made him confused. When he encountered something outside of his previous expectations he did not know what to do, or even whether he should laugh or cry.

For example: You come home and see your little daughter crying because her toy chair was broken by her little brother. What are you going to do? What I would do is first give her a hug, kiss her and laugh about the problem. Then I would tell her, "Don't worry honey, it doesn't matter. I am going to fix it for you." So you go to the garage to grab the tools you have collected over the years but you can't find your tool box. You ask your wife, "Honey, where are my tools?" The answer you get from your wife puts you in a new version of confusion and you don't know whether to laugh or cry. "Which tools?" she asks. "The ones I had in that brown box in the corner of the garage," I say. She says, "You mean that ugly box? I thought that box was trash and I threw it away when I was cleaning the garage."

This is a man who always sees himself as a strong father and husband who should be able to hide all his problems from his family and show them that they can rely on him to solve any problem. Even though he feels like crying that his wife has thrown away his precious tools he knows it is his job to laugh instead. He usually analyzes his problems privately and when he needs answers or the energy to look for them, he looks to his two most reliable sources: his autistic son and his little dog. The problem is that they can't really give him answers because they are just listeners, so he is on the lookout for another source. Finally he finds what he's looking for in one name: Oprah.

How is that?

The first time he becomes aware of Oprah is when he sees her on her show and the first words he remembers coming from her mouth, accompanied by a very friendly smile, are:

Don't worry!

You are not alone.

I am here.

I am your friend.

She is talking to someone else and is telling another story but he feels these words are meant for him and that she is talking directly to him. This name changes his life because he starts to get all the answers he needs from her—that is, from her television show. He feels that he has finally found a friend who understands him and can give him the answers he needs, like why the people he encounters do not understand him or why the behaviors they exhibit bother him.

Technically she is not even talking to him, but still he gets answers he needs while watching her show. Sometimes he gets the answer to a question he had in the past rather than the one most currently on his mind. But that's all he needs and nothing can change his mind about the reliability of this source. Even when he hears other people saying negative things about her, he is still very loyal.

I would like to thank my creator who gave us the gift of love to enhance our lives and all the necessary signs for us to feel it and enjoy the real meaning of life. Thanks to my two beautiful children, my daughter Sarvenaz and my son Pourya, who made my world more wonderful by coming into my life and making me smile whenever I think about them, and to my beautiful wife who brought them into my life and made me the different person I am today. I feel so fortunate for having my family. Thanks to the Autism Treatment Center of America in Massachusetts, who taught me about the SonRise Program and through which a mutual friend introduced me to a wonderful woman, Maryam Pirnazar, who encouraged me to write my journal and helped edit it. I am grateful for her knowledge and background and the generosity she shows by selflessly helping other people. She is the daughter of Samineh Baghcheban of Baghcheban Institute For the Deaf in Iran which helped thousands of children and families when there was no one else to turn to. Samineh Baghcheban is a legend in Iran, who after the revolution was treated very badly despite all the good she had done for our country.

And many thanks to my good friend Jan Schieberl, who spent a lot of her free time helping me write this story by correcting mistakes and typing it into the computer.

And this is the story.

THE NEW CAR

In November, 2000, after having corresponded with Dr. Marvin for two years, we came to the United States. I had heard of Dr. Marvin on a news program in my country where he was said to have had a lot of success with autistic children. We were very optimistic that he could help our son and we decided to bring him to see Dr. Marvin. When we landed in San Francisco, we were picked up by our hosts who took us to their home in Dublin, California.

We had planned to stay with our hosts the entire time we were in the U.S., which we thought would be only for a limited time while we consulted with the doctor. However, on the second day of our stay our hosts explained to us about the various types of hotels available in the area. Apparently we did not get the hint because on the third day we were told in so many words that it was customary in the United States for guests not to stay anywhere longer than three days. It was our first lesson about the culture in the new country and it was totally different from the culture we were used to. We decided then that rather than wait to be kicked out we should use the information our host had generously provided and move to a local hotel.

Our host was kind enough to give us a ride to the hotel. As he prepared to drive away he rolled down the window of his car. "I am very disappointed you are leaving so soon," he called out. "You know, it is very impolite to stay such a short time and leave on such short notice." He then sped away, the gravel flying from the speed of his smoking tires.

This sudden and unexpected move made me realize that I had to right away start providing the necessities of life in this new country on my own and make all my decisions by myself. My first decision was to purchase a car so we could drive to Los Angeles to see Dr. Marvin.

The day after our move to the hotel, after eating our breakfast and taking a little tour of the area where we were staying, we walked to a nearby bank to open a bank account. I had brought $14,000 in cash for our trip and was carrying it around in my pocket all the time. My request to open an account was rejected because I was a tourist and had no social security number and no credit card. I was told that opening an account without these things was impossible. I tried at two other banks just to make sure but even with my perfect background and perfect English I was not able to open an account. Finally, feeling very sad and disappointed, and with my expectations lowered dramatically, I walked into another bank.

As my family were having fun shopping in a big store adjacent to the bank, I walked cautiously to a clerk and introduced myself as a tourist with no social security number and no credit card. The clerk was a very nice and kind lady and gave me very exciting information about herself, that she was also Iranian, she understood my situation, and she would help me get what I wanted. Nothing would stop her, not even the lack of a social security number or a credit card.

I felt she was an angel who had appeared in my life at just that moment to help me. Opening an account was not the only way she helped me. She gave me her cell phone number and told me that I could call her if I needed help with anything else.

This situation made me think about why these days the value of a person is so often based on nationality or language or skin color, when these only make boundaries in our lives and prevent us from really getting to know other people. This is very wrong. A tourist like me with an urgent reason to travel to another country needs to have access to a regular life and the ability to use the facilities that are provided to the people of that country. He should only need to understand and follow the rules, and to use their language and their currency. I knew

English and I was using dollars, so what was the problem?

It turned out that I could only open my account because of who I met, not who I was. There is a problem with this because who I know is just a coincidence and could always be wrong. Who we are is the only truth we need to know and believe.

I left the bank with my new account and some hope that we could feel safe and that we wouldn't have too many problems on our trip.

While my family and I were walking back to our hotel we saw a blue Honda parked on the street with a For Sale sign in the window. The car looked nice and clean and when I told my wife and daughter that the car was for sale they were very excited and encouraged me to buy it.

The only problem to me was my concern about the price. Based on my experience with prices in my country this car had to be over $10,000, and it would be wrong to spend so much of our money on a car. Just to get some idea about the pricing of cars and to learn more about the rules of these kinds of transactions, since I had never purchased a car in this country before, I decided to call the number on the sign and ask the seller to come and meet me by the car so we could discuss it. While I was waiting for her to arrive, I decided that whatever price she offered, I would offer her half, so if she said $10,000, I would only offer her $5,000, and see what would happen.

Shortly after, we saw two ladies in their fifties approaching. One of them was the owner who introduced herself and her friend and opened the door of the car for me to see the inside. She said the price was $4,000. I was shocked at that price as it was much lower than I expected. I did not know what to say. I was very excited and with a big smile I accepted the price right away.

Apparently my reaction was not what she had expected. Since I had failed to negotiate she thought her price had been too low so she immediately raised it to $5,000.

To negotiate means that two people have to challenge each other with so many words and lies and try to crush each other so that each side feels they are getting more than they deserve. Why is this necessary?

I don't understand why using the truth should not satisfy both sides instead. When I had accepted her price I was very happy based on my budget and regardless of the real price of the car. That meant I believed her, but she didn't see it that way and raised the price instead.

At that point, I decided that I would just tell her the truth about why I had reacted so excitedly, so I did. After listening to my story she offered to let me buy the car for $3,500. She explained that she had asked more because she had expected to negotiate down to that price and had priced it $500 over what she had planned to accept for the car. I accepted this new price and paid her in cash and was very happy about the new purchase.

For me, it wasn't only happiness about the car. I was filled with pride and satisfaction for bringing hope to my family and proving myself to be worthy of their trust in me as a good leader and provider. I had clearly shown them that they could always count on me to take care of them.

At this point they did not know what had actually happened, they just assumed I had made a good deal and had purchased the car at a low price.

After we bought our new car, my family and I decided to celebrate by having dinner out. I chose McDonald's because it was the only name I recognized. We went inside and asked for three hamburgers with three sodas. The clerk could not understand me because I was not pronouncing "hamburger" correctly. I repeated my order several more times but he still could not understand me so he brought another employee to talk to me. The new clerk asked me what I wanted, this time in Spanish. I told them, "I don't understand Spanish. I am speaking English." I pointed to the menu board: "Three of those hamburgers, those sodas, and those fries." Then I realized that my order was option Number One on the board. I understood that I didn't have to say "hamburger" to order any more, I could just say "Number One." If I wanted three hamburgers, I would have to say "Number One" three times. When I came to my wife and kids who were sitting at a table, I couldn't tell them that the delay was because they did not understand my English. I told them that the reason for the delay was that they thought I was Spanish. I was happy with my answer to my wife. It showed her that there was no problem with me or my English, the problem was with their mistake that I was Spanish.

Then the happiness was over. My wife said, "The problem is your moustache. Because you have a moustache they think you are Spanish." I realized the problem was not over. Later that evening my wife and daughter forced me to shave off the moustache that I had worn for over twenty years with no problems. They thought that without a moustache people would speak English to me. I wasn't happy about this, but I thought maybe it was a good idea. But the problem was still not over, and in fact it was just beginning. After dinner we went to our hotel to sleep, planning to leave the next day to go to LA to see the doctor.

I woke up early in the morning and told my wife that I would go to check our car to make sure it didn't need anything, like an oil change, before our trip. I asked her to wake up the children, have breakfast, and get everything ready to leave when I came back.

At seven in the morning I asked the front desk of our hotel for the location of the nearest garage. I was given an address a mile and a half away. At the shop I met the mechanic who was a white man around sixty-five years old, skinny and short with a baseball cap and a big white moustache, yellowed from years of cigarette smoking. The first words he said to me were, "What's up, dude?" I said, "What does that mean, 'dude?' My name is not dude, my name is Ali." He laughed and said, "Oh, you are new in this country?" I said, "Yes, I am." He said, "Dude means brother or friend. I am calling you my friend." I liked that explanation and I said, "OK, dude, I just bought a used car which I want to take on a long trip with my family so I've brought it here for an oil change and to check to see if there is anything wrong with it." He said, "I like you. You are a safe man and very responsible. I am going to check the car it and do it very fast. You should have had an appointment because I am a busy man in this shop, but for a person like you I'll take care of your car first thing." I was very happy that he was giving me priority. There were no other cars or people there at the time, still I thought it was very nice of him to take care of me like a friend.

After a few minutes an older lady around seventy-five, short with glasses and a lot of poorly applied make up, showed up for an oil change. The dude said, "Hi Miss Jones, you are on time. I'll take care of you in a minute." She sat down to wait. After twenty minutes the dude came to me and asked me to follow him. First he showed me a sign at the door and asked if I knew how to read English. "Of course," I said, "very well. Like 'water' is w-a-t-e-r and even 'blackboard,' b-l-a-c-k-b-o-a-r-d. I can read everything." "Can you read this?" he asked. The sign said "No unauthorized persons beyond this door." He explained, "What that means is that it is against the law to let you come in beyond this door, but since I find you such a safe guy I am letting you in." I felt so happy for this special privilege. He took me to my car and showed me something on the axle. There was some kind of plastic cap that was torn. He told me that it would be safer to change that. (I thought it wasn't that important but since he had trusted me to go with him into an unauthorized area I decided to trust him.) I asked him, "Dude, how much is that?" He said, "Dude, forty dollars each." I had $200 cash in my pocket. Forty dollars for the oil change plus eighty for two axle caps and about ten for tax came to $130. I had enough, so I decided to have him fix it. After half an hour he came to me and said, "Dude, your car is ready. I have checked everything and you are safe to go." I said, "Thanks, how much should I pay?" "$580, dude," he replied. I was shocked: "What? Why? Forty dollars for the oil change plus forty for each cap is $120. Why $580?"

He was staring at me and looking confused. "Hey, dude, is that a joke? Forty dollars for the oil change and, dude, forty

for each axle, makes $520." He wrote it down and I saw my
mistake right away. One of those "dudes" was not "dude," it
was "two." So the axle caps were $240 each. He was right and
I had to pay $520 to the guy because the job was done. The
problem was I had just $200 in my pocket. I told the guy,
"Hey, dude, I have just $200 in my pocket. I have money at
the hotel but I have to go there to get it." He said, "Dude, I
accept credit cards or checks." "I know, dude," I said, "but
as I told you I am a tourist and do not have a check or credit
card. I have to pay you in cash. I have to go to my hotel room
and bring you the money." He said, "OK then, dude, go get
it." "I want to, dude," I said, "but I need my car to go. It is
too far to walk." He looked at me silently for a while, then he
said, "OK, dude, can you leave me something, like a driver's
license?" I said, "Dude, I have an international driver's license
and I need it to drive. How about if I leave you my passport?"
He said it was OK so I handed him my passport. He looked
at it carefully, especially the picture, and then said, "Dude,
you used to have a moustache but you don't have it right now."
"Oh, yeah," I said, "I got rid of it because my wife said that
if I shaved it people would not mistake me for Spanish." He
said, "OK, but this passport picture is not you." I said, "It *is*
me, the only difference is the moustache." He said, "You know,
dude, let me ask my partner and see what he says."

The partner was a man around seventy years old, short,
very slow, and very serious looking. He looked at the passport and looked at me a couple of times. Then he said, "No,
this is not him. This passport doesn't belong to him." I said,
"Hey, dudes, this passport *is* mine. The only difference is the
moustache. Ask someone else." That old lady, Miss Jones, was
the only someone else to ask. All three of us looked at her and
one of the dudes asked, "Miss Jones, can you take a look at
this passport?" Miss Jones, with her thick glasses, grabbed
the passport and compared the picture to me. Finally she
gave her verdict, "It has a moustache." I said "Yes, I used to
have a moustache but my wife made me shave it." "Why?" she
asked. I explained: "She thought it would be better so people

would not speak Spanish to me by mistake." "OK," she said, "but this is not you."

I had an idea. I took a small piece of paper and cut it in the shape of my old moustache and taped it to my face. She said, "That is paper." I took it off, found a black marker, colored it, and put it back on. Still, she said, "It is paper." I did not know what to do. She said, "Unless you draw a moustache on your face..." I said, "OK, but how? With a marker? How am I going to wipe it off?"

She said, "I have an eyebrow pencil that is easy to wipe off. I can give it to you." I said OK. She said, "You know, I bought it for fifteen dollars but I'll give it to you for two, because after you use it I can't use it anymore." I said OK to that too. She emptied her purse which contained makeup, magazines, keys, some cookies, etc., plus a pair of handcuffs. When the handcuffs came out we all looked at her, and she looked back at us. Finally she found the eyebrow pencil, which had been used and sharpened down to less than an inch. But I had no other choice. I asked her to help me draw it on since the result would have to be judged by her and the two dudes. I figured since they liked and trusted her I had a better chance if she did the drawing.

She drew the moustache, taking a few minutes to complete her artwork. The dudes watched intently. When she finished all three looked very seriously at my face. She began to compare my new appearance with my passport picture while the dudes' gaze was on her as the expert witness. Finally, she gave a positive verdict, "Yes, this is him." I was so surprised. Still, I got the permission to take my car to the hotel and bring the money. My problem was solved. But when I looked in the mirror to wipe off the moustache I was shocked to see that it was not at all like the moustache I had in my passport. She had drawn a Chaplinesque moustache. But who cared at this point; my problem was solved.

When I tried to wash off the moustache, however, it would not come off. "Hey, you told me it would come off easily, but it is not coming off," I said to Miss Jones. She said, "Yes, I told you it will wipe off easily if you use a special lotion, which I have. I will give it to you for another two dollars." I said fine. It did not matter to me as the problem would be solved with only four dollars.

Again she emptied her purse to find the lotion. It was a big bottle with a tiny amount left in it. I looked at her and thought, "OK, the problem is solved." I wiped off the moustache and drove back to the hotel after almost three hours for an oil change. When my wife saw me she angrily asked, "Why are you so late?" My answer was: "Because you made me shave my moustache so that I would not be mistaken for Spanish. That is why. Now let's go. Don't ask any more questions."

After another two hours we went back to the mechanic's shop to pay the rest of the money and pick up my passport. The first dude and Miss Jones were not there, but the partner was. I said, "Here is your money. Now please give me back my passport." He said, "Passport? What passport?"

"The passport I left here to go to the hotel to bring your money," I said.

"I don't know about any passport, you should ask my manager."

"Where is that dude?"

"He went out to buy something."

"When is he coming back?" I asked in frustration.

"In maybe two hours."

"Can you call him?"

He said yes but didn't do anything. "Go ahead," I said, "call him!" He said OK and called the dude who told him in which drawer to find the passport. He checked the drawer while talking to the dude. Finally he found the passport, opened it, looked at the picture, looked at my face, and said, "No, this is not him. Where is *his* passport?"

I was so frustrated. I did not know what to do and I was angry. So I just threw the money on the counter, grabbed the passport, and stormed out. As I got to the car I said under my breath, "Oh God, what do I do? Should I laugh or should I cry?"

I started driving. After two hours on the road I saw a car stopped at the side of the road with an old couple standing near their car which had a flat tire. I decided to stop and help them and thought it was a good opportunity to teach my daughter that she should always help people, especially older people. I parked my car close to them and said, "Hey guys, it looks like you need help. I can help you."

The guy said very seriously, "No, we don't need help. I know what to do!" The woman began yelling at him, "What are you talking about? We have been here for half an hour and only just now you realized we have a flat tire. Let the guy help us!" They started arguing with each other. So I said to the guy, "You know what? You have a lot of experience and you know how to do the job. You can manage me to make sure I do it correctly." (He wanted to show his wife he was still a man and could do it correctly and I thought this would help him save his pride.) He was happy to hear that and agreed to my suggestion.

But then another problem arose. He started dictating to me every single move in great detail, from how to open the trunk, where to find the spare tire, how to use the jack—everything I already knew how to do. But I myself had told him to oversee my work so I had no other choice but to go along with it. I was also trying to make the experience cheerful and fun for my little daughter so she would be happy. As I opened the trunk, I saw hundreds of small bags, suitcases, bottles, books, papers, etc. All of this I had to remove and the removal of each piece had to be orchestrated by the old man. Still I did it.

Finally I switched the tires, put the flat one in the trunk, and everything was ready to go. But the guy said, "You know, there is another problem." "What problem?" I asked.

"I don't have a spare tire right now," he said. "What if I have another flat tire along the way?"

"Go to the next city, have your flat tire fixed and then continue your trip."

"That would be Summerfield," he said.

"No, that would be Winterfield," his wife barked.

"It *is* Summerfield," he barked back.

Their argument continued until I stopped it: "Hey guys, no matter what the name of the town, just stop there and have your tire fixed. That's all!"

"OK, but you should follow us in case we have another flat," the guy said. "Then I don't have to explain to someone else how to fix the tire. You already know how to do it and I won't have to supervise you again."

I looked at my family, who were laughing, and realized I had no other choice. I said, "OK, I will follow you to the next city."

I drove behind them going 30 mph on a road with a 65 mph speed limit. Since there was no passing lane a pickup with two cowboys was stuck driving behind me. They flashed their headlights and blew their horn at me but I could not help it. I was driving behind my "supervisor." Finally we reached a place where they could pass, which they did while showing me a finger.

I did not feel bad because in my country that is not a bad finger. My daughter asked why they did that. I said because they knew we were helping some old people and showing that finger is a kind of appreciation. I was happy; those two guys were happy; the old couple was happy—who cares what really happened?

Finally we reached the next city, which was not Summerfield or Winterfield, it was Springfield. As the old couple turned off at the exit, I left them going 64 mph! Finally we got close to our destination at 10:00 P.M. We decided to stop for dinner. I saw a McDonalds sign, the only place I knew how to order by numbers without mentioning the word "hamburger." We stopped to order three orders of the meal. I asked for two orders of Number One and one order of Number Three. After a few minutes I was handed four meals. I said, "I asked for two orders of Number One and one order of Number Three." He said, "No, you ordered three orders of Number One and one order of Number Three." It must have been the way I pronounced "two" that sounded like "three" to him. So I thought in the future I will use my fingers to show how many of what I want. From language, to numbers, to fingers...

At the table my wife said, "This is too much. Why did you get this much food?" I couldn't tell her it was because the guy misunderstood me again, so I said, "I am very hungry and want to eat more." So I was forced to eat two hamburgers, two fries and two cokes which was way too much for me. Everybody was happy but the problem was not over. My daughter was not able to eat more than half of her dinner and my wife did not eat French fries to keep her shape, so as is the culture in my country, where a father's job is to finish the food of his family so nothing goes to waste, I had to eat their leftovers too. Finally we left, after I had forced myself to eat two and a half hamburgers and three and a half orders of fries. This was not very comfortable for me but I had done it so that my family, especially my wife, did not once again see that my English was not understood.

As we left the freeway approaching the city, my car broke down with a very loud sound and stopped abruptly. "What happened?" asked my wife.

"Bad news," I said. "The car is broken down."

"Then go ahead and fix it!" she said.

"I can't. The transmission's broken."

My daughter started feeling scared and said, "Dad, this is the U.S., everybody has a gun. Are they going to kill us?"

"Don't worry, sweetie," I said. "This is the U.S. Any time you stop, in a few minutes a cop is going to drive by and will stop and help you."

After twenty-five minutes, however, not a single cop passed us. I did not know what to do so I decided to try to stop another passing car to get some help. There were lots of cars driving past us.

After a while a small pickup truck stopped and I went to the driver's side window and I saw a Spanish man around fifty years old, with a moustache and a cowboy hat, with his little daughter in the car. He asked me, "What's up, Amigo?

What's the problem?" I said, "Hi, and thank you for stopping. I am a tourist and I am with my family. I need some help, I don't know what to do."

He said, "Don't worry, I will help you. Do you know why? I am from a big family. My father came here a long time ago and he taught us to help people, especially tourists. I will help you. You know, I have a cousin. He is big, too. You know why? Because he is from a big family. His father was my uncle. He is a big man. He has a tow truck. I will call him right now." He called and spoke to someone in Spanish. When he got off the phone he said, "I called him, he is going to come. His name is Eddie and he will help you." Then he drove off.

I was pleasantly surprised and filled with hope. Sure enough, shortly afterwards a tow truck came and parked in front of my car.

"Eddie?" I asked.

"Tourist?" he said.

"Yes. Thank you for coming."

"No problem. I am going to help you, my friend."

He got out of his car. He was a Spanish guy with a big moustache and small eyes, wearing a baseball hat. To be honest, I was expecting a big guy because of what his cousin has said, but he was barely five feet tall. I told him the story about the car and he said he knew a mechanic.

"I will take you there, my friend. You know why? Because I am from a big family. My father came here a long time ago and he taught us that we should help people."

As he was pulling my car onto his tow truck he went on, "You know, I have a big family and I can support them very well. You know why, my friend?"

"Because your father taught you?" I said.

"No, because I am smart, my friend," and he pointed to his head. "I never break the law."

"Wow!" I said, just to make him happy.

"Yes, I don't even have one single ticket on my record, my friend."

"That's great," I said.

As he put my car on the top of his trailer, he said, "You know, my friend, by law I can only carry two people inside my truck and I cannot carry a car with people inside it. But you are four people, my friend. This is a problem. So what should we do?"

"Maybe I should call a cab?" I wondered.

"No, my friend," he said, "two of you, like your wife and one of your kids, can ride in my car and the other two, like you and your other kid, can go inside of your car, but you should fold down your seats and lie down so nobody can see you. Then, we have done our job and we didn't break the law, my friend."

I looked at him, I looked at my car, I looked at my family and then I said, "OK, Eddie, you really are smart."

So, my wife and son sat inside the truck with Eddie, and I climbed with my daughter into my car. We reclined the seats and lay down so nobody could see us from the outside.

It wasn't a good situation for any of us, especially for me with my hurting belly, but there we were and I was not able to do anything else. So I tried to make it fun for my daughter. I would put a finger up to the window, taking a risk that we would be detected. This made my daughter laugh and making her happy helped me forget my own gastronomical problems for a while. After twenty minutes of driving we stopped and Eddie came up to me.

"Hey, my friend, the mechanic's shop is at the end of this street. If I go there and drop your car you guys will be four and I cannot carry you in my car. You know why? Because this is against the law. This is my home [pointing to his house]. This is Consuela, my wife. You guys can stay here and I will go and drop off your car at the mechanic's shop. I will be back soon."

"Thank you," I said, "that's a good idea." So we got out of the truck, taking some of our things from the car, and then he left.

Consuela was a Mexican woman with a big smile and short like Eddie. She invited us into her home in Spanish. I didn't know many words in Spanish, just "Gracias" and "Si," but we understood her invitation. We went inside. This was a very small home, a small dining room, two bedrooms, one small kitchen, and a bathroom. All the doors opened to the dining room. In the dining room were two big sofas facing each other, two loveseats, three chairs, and one coffee table. A small TV stood in the corner of the room. There were some pictures on the wall including a large picture of Jesus on the cross.

This was all I saw in that room. I noticed everything was small except for one thing, which was the number of the family members. There were a couple of older people, that I think Consuela indicated were her parents, one dog (a yellow lab), one Persian cat, and nine children who seemed between two and twelve years old. Consuela asked us to sit on one of the sofas, which was the best one in the room. All four of us sat there and the rest of the family, except Eddie who was dropping off my car, and Consuela who left us to go to the kitchen, all sat or stood lined up in front of us. Nobody said a word. Not a smile. They all just stared at us very seriously. Even the two animals were staring at us.

The situation was a little uncomfortable. I didn't know what to do. My daughter asked me, "Dad, why are they staring at us like that?" I said, "Because they are surprised to see your mom. They have never seen any other human like her on this earth." My daughter laughed. "No," said my wife. "They are staring at how beautiful I am."

I felt that I had a responsibility to break the silence, so I said to the kids, "Are you guys brothers and sisters?" I heard a couple of "yeses" and a couple of "sis" at the same time. Then silence again. I felt that my effort was not enough and I must make my questions a little more specific. So I said, "Who is the oldest?" Again a couple of the kids said simultaneously, "Juan." I didn't catch who said that or who Juan was. There were a couple of boys who looked like they could be Juan. This time I asked, "Who is the youngest?" Again everybody answered, "Rosita." Nobody changed the direction of their gaze so I still didn't know which was Juan or which was Rosita. Finally Eddie came and helped me escape from that situation. Eddie gave me the business card for the mechanic's shop. "My friend," he said. "I left your car at the shop. He is my friend and I told him to fix your car and give you a good price. Don't worry, he will take care of you and this is his card. Call him and talk to him tomorrow."

"Thanks, Eddie," I said. "This is great. You are my dude. If you could please call a cab that will take us to a hotel I will appreciate it very much."

"My friend, I am from a big family. You have to have dinner with us. This would be a kind of blessing for us."

I couldn't say that I was there already with two and a half hamburgers and three and a half French fries in my stomach and not feeling very comfortable about it as it was. I just said no thanks, that we were full as we had already had our dinner. But Eddie said, "My friend, that is OK for your family, but you are a man. You should have dinner with me." So I said OK as I felt I had no other choice.

He pointed to the bathroom, "If you guys need it, there is the bathroom."

I did all the translation for my family. They knew how much food I had already eaten and they were very amused that I would have to eat some more. My daughter went to the bathroom. To be honest, I was the only person who *really* needed to go to the bathroom to relieve my serious distress, but I knew that particular bathroom job was not going to be a simple one for me. Also, since the door opened to the dining room I decided it was not a good idea to do it then.

Consuela brought us four or five different kinds of Mexican food. She put them on the coffee table in front of me and Eddie. The rest, including the pets, sat or stood, watching every move. Consuela gave me a big plate and heaped some of each food on the plate, finishing up with two tortillas. The amount of food on the plate was enough for two adults, but in order to be polite I tried to eat anyway. The food was already quite spicy and I don't like spicy food at all. But she then added more hot sauce to my food to make it even spicier. I continued trying to eat it, drinking some water after each bite. Then Eddie jumped up and said, "My friend, don't touch that sauce! That is not for men."

He took a small bottle of something from his pocket. He shook the bottle over my food. This sauce was extremely hot and immediately burned my mouth. I felt like I was inside a pot of boiling water, waiting to be cooked. The older man told Eddie something and Eddie looked at me and said, "Yes, hold on, my friend," and he told his wife something in Spanish. Consuela went to the kitchen and came back with a big bottle that I guessed might be tequila. He poured some for himself and a little for me. I could not say that I did not want any to him, not because I am a Muslim but because I was not able to talk. With all that food in my stomach, and my mouth and entire body on fire from the hot sauce, I was in a total stupor of discomfort and pain.

When I put another bite of food in my mouth, burning hot as usual, I tried to wash it down with a glass of water. After I chugged down the entire glass I realized it was the wrong glass and that I had drunk the whole glass of tequila at once. At this point everybody was in a shock, staring at me to see what the result would be. This situation was very funny for my wife and daughter but I could not go on any longer. "Hey, Eddie," I said at first opportunity, "I need you to call a cab because my kids are tired and we need to go to a hotel." I turned to Consuela and said, "Gracias, that was delicious."

Eddie offered to let me have one of their bedrooms so that we could spend the night there. I thought to myself, "This man who doesn't even know me has already helped me a lot with my car and now he has invited me to stay at his house." I felt very grateful. This emphasized my belief that all people are the same no matter what nationality, culture, or religion, as this man who really had not much himself, still wanted to share everything he had with us.

Again I thanked them and asked him to call a cab, which he did. I tried to offer Eddie some money for all his help but he said, "No, my friend. Money is not everything."

We said goodbye to everyone and got into a cab. As we sat down my daughter said, "Hey Dad, I didn't know that Mullahs drove cabs." I looked at the driver and noticed she was not wrong. The driver was a Sikh man around thirty, skinny and short with a lot of hair on his face. He was wearing a big orange turban. I told my daughter, "No, honey, he is not a Mullah. They are Sikh and this is what they wear."

I told the driver to take us to the nearest hotel. I wanted to stay close to my car in the shop and didn't want to have to walk too far the next morning. He said, "OK, sir. Are you tourists?" I said, "Yes, we are tourists." He said "OK, sir, I will take you to a good hotel with a good price. I know them and you can save some money," and he drove off. Very shortly, at the end of the street we were on, we passed a hotel. I looked at him, but he didn't stop. I kept silent to see where he would take us. He entered the freeway and drove a few miles, exited on to another freeway, drove a few more miles, took another exit, and then went back to the original freeway.

Finally after twenty minutes we were back at the hotel which we had passed in the first minute. I looked at him and I looked at the hotel that I remembered very clearly, "Days Inn." (In Tehran where were living, there was a good hospital near us with the name "Day," so this is why I remembered it so clearly.) I looked at the meter which showed $55. I understood what he had done. So I asked my family to get out of the car and I walked to the driver's side. I gave him $5 and told him, "I know what you did. I am here because my car is broken. I am a tourist. I don't have a car. I am very uncomfortable as my stomach is full of way too much food, a big Mexican dinner with a lot of hot sauce, two and a half hamburgers, and three and a half orders of French fries. You drove me on the freeways just to make your meter go up. Do you think I am stupid? Don't make me release all my anger on your head. Take this money, shut up and leave here. I don't want to see you again. I don't want to hear a word from you."

The driver didn't say a word, looked very sheepish, said

"Sorry" very apologetically, and drove off.

I asked my family to wait outside while I went into the office. There was a Vietnamese couple sitting behind the counter. The man had round thick glasses and was mostly bald, and the woman had on a ton of makeup with a lot of hair extensions. They seemed to be around fifty years old. There was also an American guy standing next to them who was also around fifty, with a small unlit cigar in the corner of his mouth and wearing a fedora with a feather sticking out.

"Hi," I said. "I need a room."

The woman said something I could not understand so I asked, "What did you say?" She repeated it but I still did not understand. The American guy intervened, "For how many people?"

"Four," I said. The woman said something else and this time I looked at the American guy. "How many females and how many males?" he asked.

"Two females, two males."

"In each room we have just one king size bed, so do you want two rooms?"

"No, I just want one room. One bed will be fine."

"How many hours?" he asked again.

"For one day. What is your check out time?"

"You want a side mirror or top mirror?"

"What do you mean mirror? I don't care where the mirror is. Whatever is cheaper," I said.

The lady looked very happy and brought out her calculator. "That will be $800," she said.

I was shocked. "What? Why?"

At this time my daughter walked in and asked for the bathroom. I looked at the guy and asked if there were any bathrooms that my daughter could use. He pointed to the bathroom and the hotel people looked at each other. The guy said, "Do you have your daughter with you?"

"Yes, of course! I told you I am with my wife and my son and daughter. Two females and two males. I am a tourist."

They looked at each other, discussed for a few moments

and finally asked for $80 instead of $800 and said check-out time was 12:00 P.M., and gave me a key.

When I entered the room I saw a big mirror on the ceiling, a painting of a naked woman at the head of the bed, and a special chair in the corner of the room. I had seen that type of chair once before—at the gynecologist's office when I went with my wife. Then I realized what kind of hotel this was and why the discussion about the number of females, males, and mirrors. At that time I was so upset about my car, my gastric distress, and the situation we had found ourselves in that I could not comprehend what was being said. I was again in the position to ask God what I should do now: Laugh or cry?

I didn't let my family come into the room. I told them to stay outside the door and wait for me. I went to the office and told the guy, "Hey, now I understand where I am. Please, this is my family. Give me some new sheets and some unused blankets." I gave him $10. He gave me four clean sheets and two blankets that he said had never been used. He said, "Be comfortable, these are clean."

I came back to the room. I put two sheets on the floor for us to walk on. I covered the whole bed including the pillows with the two other sheets. I took down the painting of the nude woman and turned it to the wall in a corner. Now, so far so good. My wife said, "Hey Ali, look at this chair? What is that doing here?"

"Well, you know, the owners here are Vietnamese. They are immigrants and don't have that much money. They bought this hotel cheap and have furnished it with free furniture that they have found on the street. This is a chair. No matter what it looks like it still fills the corner of the room."

Then my daughter wanted to turn on the TV. I immediately jumped up and took the remote control away from her and turned off the TV. "Why can't we watch TV?" she said. I said, "Honey, we don't have that much money to pay extra for TV programs."

"You have to pay for TV here?" she asked.

"Yes, in this hotel they charge extra for everything. There

is a meter in the TV and whatever time you spend watching they charge you." To try to put a funny spin on things I continued explaining: "For example, your mom can't use the bathroom because it will cost too much."

After that I went to the bathroom to do my long awaited job, and afterwards I cleaned the entire bathroom to make sure it was safe for my wife and kids to use. I used the hotel shampoo but not the towels (we had brought some of our own towels with us). Then I said, "OK, guys, let's go to bed and sleep. We have had a long day and tomorrow I have to wake up very early."

In bed, we saw ourselves in the mirror above us. As I expected, my daughter asked why there was a mirror on the ceiling. I had no answer and no idea what to say to her so I used my regular bag of tricks. I said, "Just to remind the husbands of the monster they married, lying down beside them." My wife said, "No, it is to remind the husbands of what beautiful wives they married." "OK?" I then said to my daughter. "Now go to sleep!"

I was happy that most of our problems were now solved. After about five minutes, however, the door of our neighboring room opened and closed. Shortly after that a lot of interesting sounds started happening. This made me realize that I could expect new problems. Already I was pondering my answer when my daughter asked me about those sounds. First, I pretended to be asleep. After a few seconds, my daughter said again, "Hey dad, our neighbors are fighting."

"Yes, sweetie, they are fighting."

"Don't you want to do something?" she insisted.

"No, this is not our business. When couples have problems they like to fight."

"OK, but why do they come here to fight?"

"You know, honey, when some parents have a problem and they don't want to fight in front of their kids, they come to a hotel, have their fight, resolve their problems, and then they go back home."

"But I don't remember you guys ever going to a hotel."

"Because my problem with your mom is too huge for fights. Your mom is my unsolvable problem so we don't need to go somewhere to solve it."

My daughter laughed at that and the sounds stopped shortly after that. "OK, back to sleep now," I said.

Unfortunately that kind of problem was not over for long in that kind of hotel. A few minutes later another couple came to the next room to fight. This time the sound was a lot louder and more serious. The rhythmic slamming of furniture against the wall added to the sounds the people were making. Again my daughter said, "Dad, they are fighting again!"

This time my wife wanted to fix the problem so she said, "No, somebody is in labor having a baby in that room."

"Yes, that is right. But, Dad, why are they having a baby here instead of a hospital?"

"You know, hospitals are too expensive in this country. So people come to this kind of hotel, have their baby cheaply, and then they go home."

"Yes," said my daughter. "I noticed that the name of this hotel is the same as the hospital near our house in Tehran."

I knew the problem we were having would continue until morning and I had to do something about it. So I got dressed and went to see the American guy in the office. He was sitting outside the office smoking his cigar. I gave him $20 and said, "Hey, my friend, I am with my family including my kids. I know the situation of this kind of hotel. Can you give me a room on the second floor, somewhere in the corner, and try not to put people next to us if you can?" He took the money, put it in his pocket, and said, "Yes, wait here."

He came back with a key. We went upstairs to the last room on the floor. He opened it up and said, "The room next door is out of service, so you won't have any disturbances." I said thanks and asked for five new sheets. After he gave me the sheets I did the same thing I had done in the first room. Then I brought my family to the new room. My wife said, "This room is no different, why did you have to move us? All the rooms in the hotel are the same."

I was trying to hide something from my daughter and my wife knew what was going on, but instead of helping me... Oh God, should I laugh or cry? I explained to my daughter, "People come for having babies on the first floor and after they have their babies they move to the quiet second floor to rest. So we won't have any noise on the second floor. Let's go!"

We moved to the new room. My family went to bed and I went to the bathroom to clean it again. I think if I had stayed in that hotel for another ten days all the bathrooms would have been spotless!

I was happy that I was able to solve our problem again. We went to sleep but soon I heard noise from our neighbors again. This time the sound of the slamming furniture was extremely loud. Oh my God! I went outside to see what was going on. My neighbor's light was off and there was nobody in the room. I went to see my friend, the American at the front desk. I asked what was going on in that room. He said this hotel was bought by two sisters. When they had a disagreement they divided the hotel in two by putting up a wall. The neighbors we were hearing this time were from the adjacent hotel and there was nothing that could be done about that.

I went back to our room. By this time everyone was used to the noise and didn't ask anything. We all went to sleep.

Early the next morning I left the room to check with the mechanic about our car. He told me that Eddie had written a note for him describing what was wrong with the car. I had a broken transmission. The mechanic said, "Usually we charge $3,000 for a new transmission. But I know your situation so I am going to get you a used transmission that is almost new. Don't worry, I guarantee this. I will fix your problem for maximum $1,000. You can have your car back Saturday morning." (This was Wednesday.) I said, "Thanks, but there is still one problem. I need a car today because we have a doctor's appointment. Do you have any car you can rent to me for a couple of days until Saturday? Because I am a tourist and I don't have an American driver's license or a social security number or credit card nobody will rent me a car." "Don't worry," he said. "I know a guy who will rent you a car. He is my neighbor and I will tell him your car is here with me."

He called his friend, got a positive response, and showed me his office. This guy was around sixty years old, a little fat, with glasses and a moustache and white hair. While he was talking he was shaking a little bit. "Do you have any ID?" he asked. I showed him my passport. He looked at it and me back and forth a few times and said, "But this is not you. This guy has a moustache."

"Yes, I had a moustache but my wife asked me to shave it."

"Why?" he asked, and I explained that she thought I would be mistaken for Mexican and people would speak Spanish to me instead of English. He looked at the picture and again at me and said, "This is not you."

Oh God, the same problem I had in Dublin. I said, "Hold on." I went back to my car to get the eyebrow pencil and lotion and came back and said, "If I draw a moustache on my face I think you will recognize that the passport is mine." He said, "Yeah. OK. Let's see."

"OK," I said, "but I cannot apply it on my face myself." (I knew that if I drew the moustache I would not get his approval, but if he did it himself it would be different. I know human nature is such that if people do something themselves they think what they have done is correct but if someone else does it they think it is done all wrong.)

He started drawing his art with his shaky hand. It took about five or ten minutes until he was satisfied with his work. Then he looked back and forth from the picture to me a few times and finally said, "Yes, this is you." He gave me the car and I paid him. When I looked in the car mirror to remove the moustache you know what I saw? A very narrow, shaky broken line on each side of my nostrils, looking nothing like a moustache and more like an EKG printout—but he had liked it. What could I say? At this point, again I thought, who cares? He was happy, I was happy, I got the car, and the problem was solved. I removed the moustache with the lotion and left the shop.

Continuing our trip, we finally met the doctor. He said that if we stayed in the country for a couple of years he could do something for my son. This is all we needed to hear. We went to Disneyland, enjoyed the end of our trip, and picked up our car Saturday morning, all fixed. We were happy and very optimistic that something good would happen for our family and our life, so we decided to stay in the U.S. I knew that staying in this country would not be any problem, because I knew English very well—like water is w-a-t-e-r and longer words, too, like blackboard is b-l-a-c-k-b-o-a-r-d.

Boss Boy

The day after our return from Los Angeles, I dropped my daughter off at her new school and while walking back to my hotel I had some time to think about my situation and all the problems facing me. I was an immigrant with no job and not enough money to survive. While I was deep in my own world I noticed a Help Wanted sign in the window of a restaurant. Since I had never worked for a restaurant and did not even have a work permit, I wondered how I could get that job. But then I realized I had the answer. I had an excellent background and knew English very well and had no moustache, so why should I worry? I decided to go for it.

I walked into the fancy Italian restaurant and went up to a man in a jacket and tie. I said, "Hi my friend. I am an educated man with a perfect background, especially in management, and I am looking for a job. I saw your sign and I came in. Can we talk?"

The answer came in Spanish as he pointed to the office. I only recognized the word "manager" in what he said, so I knew he was not the right guy to talk to. I went to the office and walked in through the open door. Behind a desk sat a short, bald man with a big stomach and thick glasses who was watching the restaurant through a window. I said hi and he responded with a greeting. I asked him if he was the manager and he said he was. So I asked my question again, the same way I had asked the first guy, but this time I was asking the right person.

He asked me a number of questions, including my name, age, work experience, where I lived, where I was from, and whether I had a work permit. I answered all his questions truthfully. Then he said that there were some problems. "You don't have a work permit now BUT...!" he said with very dramatic emphasis, "you will apply for one, right?" I nodded my head in response. He continued, "You have never worked in a restaurant BUT... you know that the kitchen is the most important part of any restaurant, right?" Without waiting for my answer he continued, "You have a house and you have a kitchen in it, so you know how important the food that comes from that kitchen is to make you and your family satisfied and happy, right?" Again he did not wait for my answer. He repeated, "Isn't that right?" I nodded. He said, "My name is Luke and you can call me Mr. Luke. Although I think there is no problem for me to hire you, you should first know who I am and what kind of attitude I need to see from employees. I am very smart and I have two eyes in the back of my head," and he turned his head to show me, though all I could see was a big bald patch. "I can see everything, so be careful not to miss any part of your job. I am very organized, so don't be late and make sure you always wear clean and nice clothes, like I do." He gestured towards himself and I could see that his pants badly needed pressing. "Do you know English?" he asked. Immediately I answered, "Yes, fluently. Like, I know water is spelled w-a-t-e-r and can even spell longer words like blackboard, b-l-a-c-k-b-o-a-r-d." He looked at me in silence for a few moments and then continued, "Another thing... Never, ever tell a lie. I don't like liars or lies and I never do it myself. OK?"

I just looked at him and again I nodded. He asked, "Any questions?"

"When do I start?" I asked.

"Well, this is an elegant, high class restaurant and has strict policies. You need to have a couple of interviews with management. I was just the first one but I am probably the most important person. You know why?" Without waiting for any response from me, he continued, "Because I am the manager."

"Yes indeed," I assured him.

"Be here tomorrow at 9:00 A.M. for your second interview with the owner."

I went back home and told my wife how excited I was about what had happened and that I thought I was getting a job and would know for sure tomorrow after the last interview.

The next day I was at the restaurant at 8:55 A.M. to meet the owner, a very serious man who appeared to be around forty years old. Mr. Luke introduced me to the owner who invited me into his office while he read the information I had given Mr. Luke the day before. He looked at me periodically while he was reading but said nothing. Then he asked me the same questions Mr. Luke had asked: who I was, where I lived, etc. I answered the same way I had yesterday, but this time when I was asked about the work permit I responded with the hint Mr. Luke had dropped yesterday, that although I didn't have a work permit I would apply for one right away.

Then he asked me about my immigration status and my social security number. I replied that I was a tourist and did not have a social security number. He said, "If you apply for a work permit, this means you will apply for a green card. Then you will be a permanent resident, right?" I nodded my affirmation. "Now, having a kitchen at home doesn't really make you a good cook unless you have used that kitchen to cook. Can you cook?" I responded that I knew how to make excellent kabobs.

He then said, "You are good for work, but you should know that I am a very serious person and very smart. So never, ever lie about anything. I don't do it myself and I don't like or tolerate it in others. You also need to have one more interview with my human resources manager, which will be the last one, and then you will be hired. Of course I am the owner so when I say yes, it means yes, but you know about company policy. You can understand this, can't you?"

The human resources manager turned out to be his wife Mina, who was an Iranian woman with gold jewelry draped all over her body. I had to start with the same story again, with the same questions and the same answers, until she said, "You should know that this restaurant is very successful because of me. I am very smart and intelligent. If I wasn't watching this place, my husband would not be able to handle it and it would not be the success it is today. The world is run by women and women are the most valuable part of the world. You know why?" This time I moved my head left and right to indicate that I did not know why.

"Just look at life and the history of the humans from the beginning," she explained. "Always men were successful because of women but women always got blamed by men for anything that went wrong. Look at Adam and Eve, for example. God created man, this brainless creature with nothing but muscle. But we always hear that it was Eve's fault that they were ejected from the Garden of Eden because Eve ate an apple. Just tell me, don't you eat apples? Other people don't eat apples? Everybody eats apples. There is nothing wrong with eating apples but that poor woman ate one apple and everybody says that she was wrong. She gave birth to five kids and was responsible for taking care of her family, cooking and cleaning, and at the end of the day when she was tired and needed to rest Adam still needed something from her. Just tell me if she was not justified in eating an apple. Oh, you men!"

After she finished this lecture she added, "Just remember that I am smart and I can see everything that goes on here. You should report to me anything that happens here, OK?" I nodded in agreement.

Then Mr. Luke told me to be there tomorrow at 9 A.M. with a white shirt, black pants and a nice tie. "Your position is boss boy and you will get a good pay."

I left them with many questions still in my mind. They asked me not to lie, but they were making me lie by working there without a permit, and calling me a cook because I had a kitchen at my home, and at the end, making me even more confused by questions I had never thought about in my life. Whose fault really was it that they were ejected from the Garden of Eden, Adam's or Eve's?

When I got home I was excited that I had a job. My wife

asked me about the position and the salary. I had not asked how much I would get paid but I told her that I thought the salary would be great because this was not a regular restaurant. To be hired you had to be interviewed three times and you had to know English very well. Also, my position was that I was some kind of manager because I was told that I was a boss boy. Boss means boss, the chief person in charge, and boy must mean that I am the chief of the boys. I told her that I guessed I would be a kind of manager in charge of other employees.

The next day I prepared myself for work by wearing one of my best white shirts and black pants with a beautiful tie. Then I put three pens in my shirt pocket. Before my wife who was watching me had a chance to ask me why I had three pens, I said, "This is a very important part of being a manager, to be able to write down any mistakes I see other employees make and make notes of the rules." I left her after this and went to my new job. When I entered the restaurant fifteen minutes early I had to wait for Mr. Luke. After a few minutes he arrived and when he saw me he said, "Wow, nice clothes. Are you ready?" "Oh yes," I answered.

He called out for someone named Julio. Julio was a short and skinny Spanish guy who wore both shirt and pants that were several sizes too big for him and had a very ugly, old-fashioned tie. He said, "Si, Senor Luke?" Handing me a black apron, Mr. Luke said, "Julio, this is Ali. Take him around and show him what you do." Then Mr. Luke turned to me, "Ali, Julio is a boss boy too, so follow him and watch what he does because you will do the same job. We already have two boss boys and now with you we have three. We have ten waiters and waitresses who all service the customers, OK?" After a pause, I finally realized my mistake about the meaning of "boss boy," that it was actually "bus boy" and I was not going to be a manager after all. I said, "OK." I guessed that perhaps those pens would not be necessary.

I followed Julio who was my teacher. He took me to a table and started speaking in a combination of Spanish and

English. He grabbed a fork and said, "This is a fork. Say 'fork'." I repeated, "Fork." Then he did the same thing with a knife asking me to repeat the word. He continued with salt, pepper, sugar, napkins, etc., acting like he was a professor teaching physics at Harvard University. While I was listening to him I was thinking about how I had thought my position was going to be a manager. Now what was I going to tell my wife and daughter about my real job when I got home? But, it was a job anyway and I could make some money. Who cared what I did? Nobody knew me there and I needed to support my family.

I continued doing the job that Julio had shown me to the end of the day. The restaurant closed at 10:00 P.M. and when we finished closing Mr. Luke called me over to him. "I should talk to you about your income. Minimum pay in this state is $7.00 per hour and you should start with that, BUT [again he said the word in a very excited and loud voice] I am only going to give you $5.00 per hour. You know why?"

I moved my head from side to side to show that I had a question about it: "Why?"

"If you get $7.00 you would have to give $2.00 per hour for taxes. Taxes are a very important part of our life in this country, as they go to run the country. Taxes are the way people appreciate those who run this country. But you don't pay taxes now and you know why?" Again I shook my head. "Because you don't have a work permit," he answered. "We will keep that $2.00 and save that as a debt until you get your permit. Do you agree?"

As before, all I could do was nod my head in agreement.

"BUT... I have very good news for you," he continued. "When you get your work permit, you will get the whole $7.00 and that is not all. Every six months you will get a raise!" As he said this, his face lit up in excitement and continued, "You know how much?"

I shook my head.

"Twenty-five per hour!"

"Dollars?" I asked.

"No," he said, "cents. BUT... that is not all, all the waiters and waitresses share part of their tips at the end of the day with the bus boys and they are put here in this envelope."

He handed the envelope to Julio and Julio invited me and the other bus boy, Jesus, to sit around a table while he divided up the money in the envelope. There were a few bills but mostly coins. Julio started carefully counting it out, penny by penny. It came out to $17.35 for each person. When I tried to take my share, Julio stopped me and said, "Because I am your teacher, for two weeks I take half of your tips. This is the rule, so half of $17.35 is..." He had to stop as he did not have the answer. When I saw that he was having trouble figuring out half of $17.35, I gave him $10.00 and picked up the rest. With nothing to say, I left the restaurant and went to my car. When I opened my car door to get in, I stopped for a moment and looked back at the restaurant, thinking about what had just happened. I looked up at the sky and asked God, "Should I laugh or cry?"

Then I thought of the problem I was going to have to explain to my family, especially to my wife, what my real job was. I had thought I was going to be a manager in the restaurant. "BUT...!" I thought, even if my job is a bus boy in the restaurant, I am still a manager at home. Even though what I had to do was hard on me, especially for my ego because of what I thought of as my prestigious background, at least I had found a job and was making a little bit of money.

Camera Man

One day not too long after I started my job as a bus boy, two men and a girl walked into the restaurant at lunch time. After the waitress seated them at a table and I brought them some water and an appetizer with a nice smile, I saw that one of the men was carrying a professional camera. "That is a very nice camera you have," I said to him. "It has a 35-105 range lens which is a very good kind of lens."

"Do you know photography?" he asked.

I replied that I had been a professional photographer for a couple of years.

"Why are you not still doing that?" he asked.

"Because I just moved here and I don't know anybody," I explained. Then I asked him if he worked for television or a newspaper. He said that he worked for a newspaper company.

"Are you hiring?" I asked. "I am very interested to have a professional job but, to be honest, I don't have a work permit."

"We are not hiring photographers but would you like to work in the news?"

"Oh, yes! I have very good experience there, too!"

He gave me a phone number of someone named Maria and said to call her. He told me that to work in the news you don't need a work permit and my current job would not interfere with the news job so I could do both and make more money. I was very surprised to hear this and thanked him. On my next break I called Maria, explained how I had come to have her phone number and told her I was interested in working with her. She gave me an address and told me to be there at 2:30 tomorrow. I told her that I could not come at 2:30 because I was working in the restaurant at that time and asked if I could see her either before or after my job. She said, "Your other job is no problem, I meant 2:30 A.M. The job is from 2:30 to 6:30 A.M."

"Oh, OK," I said, "I will be there at 2:30 A.M. tomorrow."

After I finished my job at the restaurant, I went home to bring the exciting news of having found a job in the news business to my family. My wife was very curious about the job. "What kind of job is that?" she asked.

"I don't know yet. But I think either as a camera man or maybe a reporter."

"Do you know how to be a reporter?"

"Of course. Don't you remember that in Iran for three years I did this for the Army Channel? I was very good at it. It's very easy for me. I just need a little practice."

Then I turned on the television to carefully watch the news reporters. I mimicked what I saw. "How was that?" I asked my wife. But I didn't wait for her answer because I was sure I had done a great job.

At 11:00 P.M. that night I told my wife that we should go to sleep as I had to wake up in a couple of hours. In bed I was not able to sleep because I was so excited that I had found a much better job. I checked the clock every few minutes. Time was dragging on very slowly.

Humans always seem to be in a hurry to reach a destination while not taking the time to enjoy the moments that they are experiencing. One of the problems with that is that often we end up at a place that was not our intended destination.

I got up at 1:30 A.M., took a shower and, wearing my best shirt and tie again, left my home at 2 A.M. and arrived at the address Maria had given me at 2:20. In the parking lot of the news building were about thirty cars and lots of people standing around talking to each other. Every age, gender and nationality seemed to be represented. I parked my car and asked one of them where I could find Maria. Maria was an average-looking Hispanic lady wearing reading glasses and sitting behind a table writing something. I said, "Hi Maria, I am Ali."

She looked at me, said hi back and noticed my clothes. "Wow, you look good. All dressed up..." she said.

"Yes, I usually dress like this."

"OK," she said, "I have a white van in the parking lot. Go there and wait for me and I will be with you in fifteen minutes."

She kept on writing while I found her van and waited for her. As I was waiting I practiced acting like a reporter standing in front of a camera, just in case my new job was as a reporter. After about fifteen minutes, as promised, Maria came to the van and opened the door on the passenger side and asked me to get in. Then she asked me if I had ever worked on news. I told her about my experience working for three years for the Army Channel on Iranian TV and that since most of our show was news, yes, I had a lot of experience. Maria was silent for a few moments, then she said that this job was different. "Do you know English?" she asked. "Can you read?"

"Sure, very well," I said "Try me." I offered her my samples. Again she looked at me curiously, then said, "OK, let's go."

As she drove she continued to tell me about the job. I would be paid cash so it didn't matter that I didn't have a work permit. The job was seven days a week, no days off, from 2:30 A.M. to 6:00 A.M. One route would make about $500 a month and if I could handle more than one route, she could give me another so I could make even more. "Any questions so far?" she asked. "No, everything is clear," I said.

Maria turned onto a street and stopped the car, gave me a folder and told me to read it. When I looked at the first page I could see that it was filled with addresses and directions.

"These are just addresses," I said.

"Yes, read it."

I read: "Turn left on Jenson Street, number 1201..."

Maria stopped me. "Now, there are two ways of doing the news. One is that you roll it and put a rubber band on it. If it is raining you put it into a plastic bag." She grabbed a paper from behind her seat, rolled it with a rubber band and said, "Now, what was the number of that house?" "1201," I said. She showed me how to throw the paper at the house and then she asked, "What is the next one?" I looked at her, I looked at the house, and I looked at the address. "1205," I said. She threw another paper at the next house. Then another and another and another, except now she was talking nonstop explaining the job. I was looking at her mouth but hearing nothing, just thinking about how what I would be doing was nothing at all like what I was expecting. I was also thinking about the other problem of what I was going to tell my wife about this new job. But most urgently I had a question: Should I laugh or should I cry?

After I finished my job training with Maria she dropped me at my car and asked me how I liked the job. "I know for now it is hard," she said, "but you should know we are delivering news to people to help them handle their lives better. This is a very important job. So see you tomorrow."

"For sure," I said.

While I was driving back to my house time seemed to be rushing by very quickly even though I was driving only fifteen miles in a forty mile per hour zone. The reason for driving so slowly was that I didn't yet know what I was going to do when I saw my wife and daughter, or what I was going to say. Through my mistake I had built a very different expectation in their minds (and my own) about the job. Last night I was suffering because time seemed to be moving so slowly. Since then nothing had changed except my expectations. Last night my expectation was all wrong but I was in a big hurry to reach it. Today my expectation was real but I was not interested in reaching it at all.

When I realized that what was really important was that now I had another way to make a little more money for my family, I relaxed a bit and felt less anxious. So all I had to do was tell them the truth. I was not doing anything wrong. I was someone in my own country but over here nobody knew me. Why should I keep having these wrong expectations? Taking care of my family and raising my children is the most important job for me now. Yes, I will just tell them the truth.

At home my wife and daughter were having breakfast.

They looked at me expectantly, waiting for me to tell them about my new job. I looked back at them for a moment and then I only said, "$500 a month."

Silence. They kept looking at me. "Three hours a day, seven days a week. Cash," I said. More silence. Nothing changed in their faces as they waited for me to tell them more about the job. So I added quietly, "As a cameraman."

What I saw in their eyes was not really satisfaction, but it was OK. At least it was better than telling them I delivered newspapers. When I left them to take a shower I was not happy about having lied to them. But why should I tell them the truth when it wouldn't change anything. They needed my support and when I was out of their sight I was doing a legal job for people. They were still satisfied with me as a strong leader. That was enough.

This was our start in this new country for the first year until I got my work permit. I still had the dream of finding the best job for me, one that would use the skills and abilities I had acquired through my life, the job I deserved to have given my wonderful background.

That first year I had many difficult times working in the restaurant as a bus boy and delivering newspapers. People looked at me as a nobody, a simple person who could only handle these simple tasks. This bothered me very much and I was not able to share my feelings with anybody, not even my wife. I could get no relief from my frustration. I had to hide my pain. I only had my beautiful autistic son to listen to me with no judgment when there were just the two of us together. He was my only source of relief from the problems in my life. By looking at his beautiful eyes I was able to get the energy I needed to get me through each day.

Oh my God, how love reveals its true meaning when you really find it. It helps you forget the small and unnecessary problems humans create in their lives. I talked to my son for hours and hours the way best friends do. What I got back was the strength to go on.

COURIER

After applying at the immigration office and waiting over a year I was finally a legal temporary permanent resident with a work permit. I was very excited about this because it meant I could get better jobs more suitable to my skills, background and, mostly, my prestige. I was disappointed so far with this country and the regulations that made me useless to people who could have appreciated my values and my work.

In Iran a lot of value is placed on relationships and meeting and talking to others in person. Papers and documents were not that useful in getting what we wanted or needed. Very infrequently did we receive anything in the mail. This country was different and using paper was very important for communication, advertising, or just acquiring the necessities of life. I remember shortly after I was approved to stay in this country as a permanent resident, I began to receive a lot of mail from different companies and banks. This was very surprising to me but I was very happy to think that finally my wonderful background and who I was as a person was being acknowledged by the society in which I was living. I took all those letters very seriously and tried to figure out why they were sending them to me. Most of the letters were offers to improve my life by providing financial "strategies." What made me happiest was to see that suddenly I was approved by banks, without even asking or applying, to get whatever cash I wanted right away with no, or very minimal, interest.

But the problem was that reading and responding to all those letters took up a lot of the little free time I had. I wanted to carefully consider each offer so I devised a filing system for answering each letter quickly and efficiently, and keeping track of them. I didn't want to miss a single one. The result was that I ended up with ten different credit cards that created new problems in my life, as I was soon deeply in debt. I had felt that not answering those letters offering me financial assistance would have been rude. Eventually I learned that some of the things that appeared to be offering help were really adding more problems to my life. I realized that the lifestyle offered by those offers was putting people in debt for the rest of their lives. If we had never received those letters in our mailbox we would have managed our needs with what we had and would have been able to make our way based on our own abilities. This lesson was not a comfortable one to learn but once I realized how dangerous those letters were I would just dump them in the garbage as soon as they arrived. I felt bad that so much paper was wasted instead of being used in the right way. I was only happy when mail from real friends arrived or important official letters like my long-awaited work permit.

The arrival of the work permit was a big event in our family and as soon as I received it, I bought a newspaper to start looking for my next job.

My wife had many other urgent questions, however. She wanted to know where we were going to buy a house and how many cars we were going to buy. She wanted me to buy her a ring with a large diamond on it. Even my daughter had a lot of ideas for spending money which we did not yet have. She came out of her room with a list of the things she wanted, including new clothes and shoes and even which breed of dog she wanted.

As I was surrounded by these questions and requests the only person in my home who did not have a wish list was my little son Pourya, who was happy by himself in his own world. His world was a beautiful world in which he could only see what was real. In it he was happy with what he had, who he was and who I was, and not what I might buy for him.

Around this time I began to be aware of the fact that autism is not the kind of disability we had thought it was.

Technically, a disability is when a person cannot do what they need to do or understand what they need to know. Autistic people are not disabled in this way. Of course not. They just haven't had the proper training because we have not yet found the key to enter their world and to teach them what they need to know. I believe that in some ways they know everything very well. I think they know even better than most of us because they view their world with a pure sense of humanity and love. This is what I sensed in my son. I felt lucky to be familiar with his beautiful world and I was thankful to God for bringing Pourya into my life and letting me see the world from his eyes. This changed me totally from the person I was. I found that if I wanted to help him I first needed to enter his world with no judgment and then look for the problem.

After my wife and daughter finished telling me what they wanted, first I told my daughter that there would be no dog. We are Muslim and cannot have a dog in the home. Why? I don't know but that was what our religion teaches and to honor our religion we had to follow its rules. "As for the rest of your list," and I turned to my wife, "and yours, give me time to first find a job. Once I have a good job it will still take time to make some money before we decide how we are going to spend it." Then I kissed them both and my son, and sat at the table to look in the newspaper for my next job. I focused on management positions with high salaries and good benefits.

I found listings from a courier company by the name of Bird for several different positions. One was as a supervisor and required a master's degree in management, which I had, and at least five years' experience, which I also had. I had even more than five years' experience in the Iranian Air Force as an officer and commander. I called the company and gave them the good news that I was the person they were looking for. They gave me an appointment for an interview with someone named Nadia George who was the head of the company.

On the day of the interview I wore my best suit, the same one I had worn when I first met Maria for my job with the newspaper. Bird Company had a big office with a couple of employees working busily at their desks. The first person I saw was a large black lady in her early thirties with no makeup and so much hair that it was tied with a band in the back. She was dressed all in black and did not look happy at all. In fact, she looked pretty angry. I said hi, introduced myself, and asked for Nadia George. She wordlessly pointed to an office where I found a very good looking lady, also in her thirties, dressed very nicely, sitting at her desk. I walked into her office with a very charming attitude and was received with a beautiful and warm smile. She asked me for my resume. I had written out my resume by hand as I did not know how to type on the computer. She read it with a positive attitude and asked to see my documents proving my degree. I explained that I did not have my documents with me as I had not planned on staying in the U.S. I told her that the reason we had come here was to get treatment for my son and go back directly but it had turned out that he needed to stay here longer.

She asked about my work experience. "You have never worked in the U.S. as a manager, have you?"

"No," I said.

"So how can you prove you are who you say you are and that what you have written in your resume is true?"

"By my word and my ability, which I am going to prove to you when I start my job in this position."

She looked from my resume to my face back and forth a few times in silence. Then she said, "I am sorry but I can't give you the job based on just your word." After a pause I asked, "OK, so what kind of position can you offer me in my situation?" She looked at me briefly and said, "There is only one position available to you."

The next day I started my new job in a company uniform as a courier. My job was to deliver mail using my own car. I was supposed to be happy with a new job with better pay and some benefits and the opportunity to be a supervisor–at least, at home I was supposed to be happy in front of my wife and daughter with whom, once again, I had not been completely honest. At home I had to pretend that I had landed a supervisory position because this is what my wife and daughter expected of me. I had planted the idea in their heads myself. At the new company I had two days of training as a simple delivery man. My job was to pick up and deliver mail for different businesses and banks. I was assigned a route in my own area. I drove back and forth, meeting a connection person who reviewed the mail I collected and handled the mail that I delivered. Of course my education and background so far had not helped me get a better job, but still they helped me perform my job better than others. My ability to excel at the job was clear so after only six months I was promoted to a new position called "Gold Seal" which had better pay. This title was usually earned after two years of a courier proving himself trustworthy and competent. What the Gold Seal position entailed was the delivery of important materials such as checks or documents that needed to be delivered quickly and safely.

I drove about 350 miles a day all over the San Francisco Bay Area. I had a one-hour break for lunch which I took wherever I happened to be at the time. Sometimes when I was close to the office I would have lunch in its kitchen which was equipped with things like a microwave oven and refrigerator. I sat at the table and enjoyed the music and books or newspapers provided by the management. This job was not very hard and I had just three to five deliveries a day. During my break I had to inform the dispatcher, a large man with a big stomach named Bill, that I was taking my lunch.

At my company I gained a reputation as a good worker with a friendly personality who could get along with everybody. Most everyone had a good attitude and we all got along well together, calling each other by our first names and having fun by telling jokes or making pleasant conversation. However, that first person I encountered at the office, Jackie, was the only person who acted differently. She never smiled and was not friendly to anybody. I tried to treat her like everyone else and would greet her with, "Hi beautiful," or tell her she looked very nice. Sometimes I was rewarded with the tiniest of smiles, but that's all.

One day I happened to take my lunch break at the same time as Jackie in the kitchen. I was reading a book as I ate. After I don't remember how long Jackie broke the silence by asking me a question: "Ali, do you really think I am beautiful?" And after a couple of seconds she added, "And sexy?"

"Of course you are beautiful, Jackie," I answered. "But not sexy. Because to be sexy you should think sexy and wear sexy clothing and makeup and you should have a beautiful and sexy smile on your face all the time. But be careful, Jackie, or all the guys will fall over with heart attacks!" I saw a smile on her face at this which made me happy and I felt satisfied with myself. I was going to continue the conversation by telling her my belief that beauty is a gift that comes with us when we walk into this world but usually we don't see that in ourselves. But just because we don't see it, it doesn't mean that we don't have it. Also we don't really know what beauty means to others. But before I had a chance to continue the conversation Bill called me and wanted me to make a pick up. I left Jackie with the smile on her face to do my job.

My daughter Sarvenaz was finishing high school at that time and preparing herself for college. One evening at home, while I was having my favorite dish, *ghormeh sabzi,* I asked her about her plans for college. "Are you ready to be the next doctor in the family?" I asked her. (It should be noted that to most Iranian parents the only acceptable careers for their children are medicine and engineering.) Before Sarvenaz had a chance to answer me, I added, "If you get accepted at a good university I will get you anything you want." "Anything?" she asked. "Anything," I said. "I want a Yorkie," she said. "Anything," I said again.

A few days later she came home with exciting news. "Dad, I have gotten accepted to a few different colleges and I have chosen San Francisco State University. I want to study biology."

This was really exciting news for my wife and me. I gave her a big hug with a couple of big, noisy kisses on the cheek, just to annoy her, and said, "Now tell me what you want as a reward." She looked at me and said, "I told you before, I want a Yorkie." "Oh, yes, I remember," I said. "Let's go get one for you." She gave me a big smile. "But we can't get one just like that. We have to order it first."

"Order it? Why can't we just go to a store like Best Buy and pick one up...?"

She stopped me with, "You said I can get what I want, right? Well, I want a Yorkie and I must order it. OK?"

"OK," I said. "Here's my card. Go ahead and order it."

She grabbed the card with another kiss for me and sat at her computer to order her prize. I had already forgotten what it was called.

Three days later she came to me very excited that her order had arrived and she needed a ride to the airport to pick up her package. We drove to the airport, produced our receipt and waited for our order. I expected a small box with a new cell phone, an iPad or some other electronic device, because my daughter like other kids at her age was always asking for a new gadget. The electronic devices had different names or shapes but they all did the same thing, which was to make her talk to her friends for hours and drive up our phone bill.

Finally the clerk came out with a large and unusual box in his hands. It was wrong to call it a box, it was a cage. He gave it to my daughter and when she looked inside she jumped for joy and let out the loudest and most painful shriek I had heard in my life. She showed me what was inside and said, "Hey, Dad, this is Roscoe."

"Roscoe" was the name she had chosen when she ordered it. All I could say was, "Oh my God. It's a DOG!"

I was shocked. Nothing could have made me more upset, not even if it had been my mother-in-law delivered to me in that cage. I now would have a dog in my home. The only thing that I knew about dogs was just that these animals were named "dog." My daughter had taken advantage of my pride in her accomplishment and tricked me into bringing a dog into my home and I couldn't say a word to oppose it. I had given her my word. The only thing I could do, which is exactly what she expected, was to say, "Oh, yes. So cute! Enjoy his company!"

Roscoe was a very tiny and cute male puppy who totally changed our life. At the beginning I followed him around the house so that he wouldn't pee somewhere or damage the furniture. I was very surprised to learn, after all my concern about having a dog in the house, that his presence was more responsible for the joy in our household than anyone else's. He would pee just outside our door but if we were too busy to take him out he would use his special pads. He appreciated the food and attention we gave him. He brought us so much joy just watching him play and he loved everybody. He was another source of support for me by quietly and non-judgmentally listening to me. When I wasn't able to talk to my son, who wasn't with me all the time, I could tell Roscoe my problems and he would just listen.

Roscoe made me think that perhaps the reason our religion does not like having a dog in the house is that after knowing how wonderful this creation of God is we would not share our lives with just other humans. Humans come to us with unreasonable expectations and unappreciative attitudes. Roscoe has brought so much happiness to everyone without expecting anything in return.

Back at the office I began to notice that Jackie had started to wear different clothes and makeup. One day when she was wearing a nice dress and her hair was made up in an attractive style I said, "Wow, Jackie, you look beautiful! I don't see any other girl in this office more beautiful!" The rest of the girls in the office said "Oooooohhhh" and some asked, "Ali, not even me?"

When I went to the kitchen to have my lunch that day Jackie joined me. I was busy as usual with lunch and my book. Soon Bill called out to me, "Ali, are you done with your lunch? I have a job for you." "OK," I said, "let me go to the restroom and wash my hands first." Then I left Jackie and the office for my assignment.

Two days later at lunch time again I came to the office

and went directly to the kitchen. As I walked in I saw something that scared more than even a Halloween horror movie. I saw Jackie with a *huge* hairstyle and way too much makeup and eye shadow. She was wearing a short, tight red skirt that showed a lot of leg and a red blouse so tight that most of her breasts were bulging out. She teetered toward me on very high heels with a big smile on her face. I was already inside the office and could not escape, so after a couple of seconds of silence I managed a "woo hoo" but it was not enthusiastic. When I sat down to lunch she sat next to me and started asking questions in a very sexy voice.

"Hey, Ali, how do you like the way I look?"

"Beautiful," I said, raising my eyebrows.

"What about sexy?"

"Oh yes, very," I said. I decided to end the conversation by turning to my book and continuing with my lunch.

"Ali," she started again, "I heard that guys from your country in the Middle East like American girls. Is that true?"

"Oh, yes," I said, continuing to eat my lunch and reading my book.

"Ali, I know you are married but it is OK sometimes to be with another girl, especially with someone you know and need to be with. I know that you would like to be with me. I got that feeling the last day that we talked. My answer is I am available whenever you need me because I think I like you."

I was staring at her mouth trying to understand what she was talking about. When she finished I stumbled, "What last day...?"

"The last time we were having lunch together I saw you spying on me. It turned you on so much that you had to go to the restroom to satisfy yourself."

"Satisfy...?"

"Yes. Then you came back to the office with your face all sweaty and asked for a napkin to dry your hands and face."

I was shocked. I flashed back to the day when Bill had called me for an assignment and I had gone to the bathroom to wash my hands and face. There had been no paper towels in the bathroom so I had to dry myself with a napkin in the office—and she thought…? Oh my God. I did not know what to say. I just said, "Thanks, Jackie, but as you said, I am a married man and I am loyal to my wife and I cannot accept your offer." I left her in the kitchen and went to Bill in the office.

"I am done with lunch, Bill. I'll wait for your call in my car." I saw the people in the office looking at me strangely and silently following me going out the door with their eyes.

Bill called after me in front of everyone. He was holding a bottle of liquid hand soap: "Try this, Ali, it works better." And he burst into loud and ugly laughter. Everyone in the office joined him. It was obvious that they were all familiar with Jackie's story. I just gave them a silent look and left. When I opened my car door I looked toward the office and thought about what had happened. Then I raised my eyes to the sky and asked, "What should I do, God? Laugh or cry?"

After this incident I decided not to eat my lunch at the office any more. A week later I dropped off a package in the city of Concord. I had parked my car in front of a funeral home and on the way back to the car I noticed a sign, "In Memory of John Smith." People were walking into the chapel. It was noon and I had time. I had a dress jacket in my car so I changed and followed the people going inside the chapel. I knew what to do there… Cry. That is what is expected at funeral homes. Inside, most of the seats were taken and a lady was talking in front and, of course, everyone was crying. I told myself this is exactly what I need. I grabbed a couple of tissues, courtesy of the management, and found a place in the second row. A black lady in her thirties with a cute little three- or four-year old boy in a little suit and tie was listening to the talk about the deceased Mr. Smith. I sat with my Kleenex in my hands, preparing for my mission of crying. After many years of wondering I finally knew whether to laugh or cry.

Listening to the talking lady and waiting to cry didn't get me in the mood for a good cry. But I wasn't a person to give up so easily—maybe the next person would do it. The next person was a large man with a big stomach and a big white moustache and thick reading glasses. He stood behind the podium with his notes and started by saying that John Smith was a good friend of his and was always there when he needed him and Mr. Smith had helped him every time he had asked for help.

All of a sudden a sound came from him, which stopped him for a moment. He glanced at the audience and shifted the podium a little to pretend that the sound had come from somewhere else other than his belly. For a moment the chapel was silent, but then he began to speak again.

The little boy sitting next to me looked at his mom and said in a loud and excited voice, "Mom, Mom! That was him! Mom, that sound came from him! He did a fart!"

The speaker looked angrily at the boy and tried to continue his speech. The mom tried to quiet her child by saying "Shhhhh" to him. This worked for a couple of seconds but then the little boy again spoke out in a voice loud enough to be heard by the whole chapel, "But neither you nor anybody else is yelling at him. When I did that at Patrick's birthday party you yelled at me. Why? What is different? How come nobody said anything when this man did it?"

This was a little boy who needed an answer but his mom again tried to make him be quiet. I decided to say something to him, thinking I might be able to help the situation.

"You know," I said softly, "you are right and that was him but you know when someone has just lost a friend or someone he loved he is sad, and when someone is sad he needs to cry to help himself relieve the pressure which is bothering him, right?"

He nodded his assent.

"OK," I continued, "but when someone has a speech to give and he cannot cry and talk at the same time, sometimes that is the only way to relieve the pressure on him to be able to continue to speak. So In this case, it is OK and no one needs to blame or yell at him. But at Patrick's birthday party you were not sad and you were not speaking in public, so you had no reason to make that sound. OK, buddy?"

After he heard my explanation, he turned to his mom and asked, "Is that right, Mom?"

"Yes, that is true," said the relieved mom.

The little boy quieted down and continued listening to the speaker. His mom glanced at me in appreciation and mouthed a silent "thank you."

The next speaker walked up to the podium and said nice things about John Smith too. Then he stepped down for the next person.

My little friend looked at me and asked, "Didn't that man love Mr. Smith? Didn't he have any pressure to relieve?" Again his mom tried to make him be quiet, while looking at me as if to say, "You started this, now you finish it."

I thought for a few seconds about what to say to this curious young boy. "Of course he loved Mr. Smith," I finally said. "Everybody loved him, that's why we are all here. And of course he had pressure too because of that, but he was skinny and when a skinny person releases pressure it doesn't make a loud sound, not like a person with a big stomach." I looked at him to see if this new explanation was convincing.

He stared at me for a few seconds and then turned to his mom excitedly, "Yes, Mom, he's right! Do you remember when my little sister Debby was in your stomach and you had a really big stomach? One night at home we were watching TV and you farted and Dad said 'your mom exploded' and we all laughed."

His mom said "SHHHHHH" to him again and this time when she looked at me I saw embarrassment in her eyes instead of gratitude. I looked at her with understanding and tried to indicate that she shouldn't worry about what the boy had said. I closed my eyes and shook my head left and right.

The funeral director asked if there was anyone else who wanted to say something about Mr. Smith. A sixty-ish man with a big belly sitting in the row in front of us stood up and walked to the podium. Standing behind the microphone he took some notes from his pocket that appeared to be two or more pages. He adjusted the mike, placed his notes on the podium and looked at the people who were waiting expectantly for him to begin. Suddenly he looked in our direction, fixing his eyes on me and the little boy. He glanced at his belly and then back at us. After doing this a couple of times he seemed to grow a little angry. He said, "John Smith was a very, very good man and I loved him a lot and I have a big stomach..." He stopped talking and stared at me and the little boy. "That's all," he said. He collected his notes and without reading them left the podium, the whole time not averting his gaze at us.

So my time at the funeral home came to an end and I still had not been able to have a good cry. I left the chapel to go back to my job. As I buckled my seat belt I looked back at the chapel and then at the sky. "Tell me, God," I asked. "What should I do...? Laugh or cry?"

THE BRITNEY SPEARS CONCERT

Moving to United States had exposed me to a lot of different things, including the way kids behave when they become teenagers. Here teenagers were far more free than they were in Iran. It was obvious that my teenage daughter wanted to be like her American friends and do all the things they did, like going to the cinema or concerts with friends. I was not happy about this and was not comfortable letting her do it. But stopping her and not letting her enjoy entertainment activities with her friends also felt wrong to me. So I decided to let her go, but only if I went with her. Then I could be happy knowing that she could enjoy herself while I was there to protect her from any trouble she might get into.

One of those times was when one of her favorite singers, Britney Spears, was giving a concert in our area. I decided to treat her to that. I was so proud to bring my daughter the wonderful news that I was going to buy tickets so that she and I could go to the concert together.

Her reaction to this wonderful news, however, was very disappointing. She was not at all pleased and told me that while she would be happy to enjoy the show with her friends, going to the concert with her father did not appeal to her at all. So, to make her happy, I suggested that she find out if another friend of hers was also going and that I would take them both. She smiled happily and said she would talk to her friends.

The next day she brought me the wonderful news that I had her approval and permission to buy the tickets. But the news became a big surprise to me when it turned out that she had invited three friends along and I had to buy five tickets.

This had not been my intention. I had thought I would be picking up a friend, who already had a ticket, and we would just go together. But I couldn't deny her wish so I ended up spending two weeks of my income for tickets to see Britney Spears.

On the day of the concert my daughter and I picked up her friends at their houses. The girls' behavior surprised me and made me wonder if these kids had not seen each other for a very long time and were overjoyed to meet once again. Their loud screaming must have meant to impress upon each other how much each was missed by the others. Apparently this was the way teenagers greeted each other.

I don't think it is necessary to explain the suffering I went through with four teenage girls in a small car, all talking at the same time, their squealing voices at the highest possible volume and pitch. It reminded me of my experience as an officer in the battlefield when I was doing my job during the war between my country and Iraq.

After spending what seemed like a few hours, first looking for a place to park and then finding our seats, we finally took our seats and waited for the concert to begin. There were thousands of people at the concert, most of whom were young teenagers my daughter's age. I was shocked to see the way the kids were dressed. Most of the young boys were wearing pants that were so big and hanging down so far that they needed to use one of their hands to keep them from falling completely off. They wore their jackets half off, with only one arm inside a sleeve. Some had shirts that were bunched up around their necks because they didn't put their arms through the sleeves. Many of them had pins and rings all over their faces. I thought they must have been running late getting ready for the show and didn't have time to put their clothes on properly but later realized that this was the new fashion.

After an hour sitting in our seats and waiting for the show to begin, Britney Spears finally appeared on the stage with her group of backup singers and the music began. I was horrified that her fans behaved so shamefully by screaming, crying and yelling during the entire three hours of her concert. I guess this was their way of showing approval and support. I don't know if anyone was listening to anything she was singing. As I said earlier, I was a pilot and all pilots train extensively to have a strong and healthy body, including ears. I had excellent hearing but as I was watching these kids, who seemed to be listening while bouncing up and down like a diving board that someone had just jumped off, including the group of girls I had come with, I began to wonder if something was wrong with my hearing. Their movements seemed to indicate that there was a song with words and a melody going on to which they were dancing. They all seemed to know the songs but I could not understand a word.

However, in order to make sure that I would be able to accompany my daughter at future concerts or any other place I might need to be with her to ensure her safety, I decided to join the girls and do exactly what they did. Those three hours were some of the most painful in my life and I hoped I would never have to endure that kind of situation again.

When the concert finally ended my head and body throbbed as I drove and dropped off each girl at her house. But the throbbing in my head continued the whole night, long after I went to bed.

After some time, when most of the memories of the concert including the pain from the horrible screaming, the unpleasant bouncing up and down for no reason, were forgiven, there was one thing I could not stop myself from being upset over in my heart. This was that I was not able to use my English skills to enjoy the words of the three hours of songs. I did not like this because I knew English very well. You know, water is w-a-t-e-r and harder words like blackboard...

DIVORCE?

After two years of living in the United States, I was struggling with my wife. She was not enjoying living with me and was not accepting me for the person I was. While I had thought that we had a strong sense of love and trust between us, this was not the case. There seemed no more hope to continue to build a reasonable life together when there was no more trust. All I had seen from her in the past were lies when she pretended to be happy with me. I believed that our life together would begin with attempts to create love between us by caring for each other and being responsible for each other. I thought that this would create trust. I had believed this and had tried to behave this way from the beginning with my wife and I had tried to solve with this feeling and attitude all the obstacles we encountered. But what I saw and heard destroyed everything in my mind and heart.

Having an autistic child at home and having to start a new life in the U.S. were not easy for either of us, but this was part of our life now and we could not blame each other for what we were not able to have. This was not what I expected and for a couple of months I was very upset with the situation and unhappy when I was home with her and this somehow prevented me from continuing to try to build our new life and trying to provide a good future for us and our children.

Divorce in human life means to give up, loss, and some other definitions that I didn't know at all. Even though, as I said before, I knew English very well, I didn't know everything. Divorce is like a shield that we use to cover our mistakes and that allows us to say that the person we had chosen to share our life with was not the right person after all and we should find another one, and maybe another and another. I felt that with the situation I had, there was no other choice for me but to think about divorce.

In Iranian culture divorce is not as common as here. I think this is partly because divorce is not used as an option to solve marital problems. This means that sometimes a couple will be forced to continue an unhappy life together, but at other times it encourages them to try to overcome difficult situations. In my experience the passing of time is the only thing that removes some problems. Also, in Iranian culture children are the main concern in a relationship, more so than in American culture, and as we know, children are happier and more successful when their parents remain together.

I knew my son was a person who couldn't understand why people, including his parents, argued and what about. In his world those topics of discussion have no value and life has more meaning when we enjoy our relationships. Love, real love, was the only sense he had for everyone in his beautiful heart. He had the right to have in his life both parents who had brought him into this world and who were responsible for all his needs. Divorce would mean that we would be thinking only about ourselves and forget our responsibility toward him. So I decided I had to disregard all the problems created by my wife and forget about what I needed for my own happiness and just focus on the happiness of my son. It was not very easy for me. Not having my desires met in life, as a man or even as a person who has a right to have the things he wants, was not what I liked. But I had no other choice. Life went on several months this way and time passed.

When a person knows that there is no real hope, complaining becomes useless and they have no choice but to finally accept their situation and see it as not really important. They realize they should place more value on caring about who they love and direct their desires to be compatible with those feelings, and this automatically brings them to a new and wonderful way of life that brings more happiness. This is what happened for us.

A prison is usually considered a punishment, but I don't agree with this. I think prison is a place for a person to think about who he is and what he has done, to discover the truth. Several times in my life I felt myself in a prison: when I was a kid and worried about what I needed to do for my mother who really needed me, when I was in the military and the people of my country needed me to protect them against the enemy, and when I saw myself as a man who had a wife and children to care for. All those times I felt I was in jail but my jail was not made with iron bars. I was surrounded by the bars of responsibility which stopped me from being free to do what I wanted to do. The last several months, while I had been in another jail, had given me the chance to think deeply about what was the real meaning of life and what exactly I needed to get from my life to be satisfied. In our moments of struggles we spend our time reaching for things that are not meant for us at those times. We don't want to accept the truth. We fight with the enemy inside in the dark. To me, being in that jail gave me the chance to find the truth to be a free man as I am right now.

Now I can say that I am really happy and satisfied with what has happened, and grateful that I had the patience to pass through those hard times. Now, having my wife, who I love even more than before and who provides hope all the time in my home which is the most important job that she has, is a blessing—even when she still criticizes me for the way I wear my clothes or for not keeping the home or kitchen neat enough. We are happy for what we have and try hard together to get the other things we need.

Even though I still don't know the exact definition of divorce in English, I am happy that I know other words and their correct pronunciations, like water is w-a-t-e-r and harder ones...

The School

We enrolled our son into the program that our county has for special needs children. Pourya went to school on the bus every day. He loved going to his school and he loved riding the bus.

Frequently I would go to the school with no previous notice, to check up on my son and what was going on at the school. I wanted to see what he was doing and how people treated him. I was very concerned about what his life would be like without me to take care of him.

On this day, I walked into his classroom and saw a number of autistic children with varying degrees of abilities. Some were walking around and playing with each other, but my son was seated in the corner of his classroom behind a desk. He seemed to be trapped in his seat since other chairs had been placed around him so that he could not move. I asked the teacher why he was put that position but I didn't get a satisfactory answer. Instead I got a very painful feeling that my son would not have the life he deserved after I could no longer take care of him. So, I gave him a big hug and took him out of school and kept him with me for the rest of that day.

For a couple of days I was very angry and frustrated with his situation in the world. I blamed everybody for having an autistic son, regardless of their responsibility or who they were. I didn't know what I should do. I had taken classes in my country to improve my knowledge about how to care for and teach my son, but nothing seemed to help and I didn't know what else to do.

I had been doing everything I could think of. I volunteered frequently in the classrooms where my son was a student so I could be around him. I stopped smoking and started exercising more so I would be around as long as possible to take care of him. But this didn't seem to be enough. What else should I do?

I was worried about this situation all the time, even when I was asleep, which wasn't often because my stress kept me up a lot of the time. When I did sleep I would frequently wake up in the middle of the night from a nightmare of finding Pourya alone in the world without anyone to care for him.

One day when I had finished my job of delivering mail to a customer, I found myself at the Golden Gate Bridge. This was around noon on a very cloudy and cold day. I parked my car and walked to a lookout point where I sat watching the bay and nature with a cup of coffee in my hand. As a Muslim I am required to pray, so at this time I decided to pray and ask God to help me. After I finished the process of preparation for prayer, which included washing my face and hands, I started to pray. I don't know the reasons for all these customs and I don't really know if I prayed the right way or not, but I did my best and at the end, I started to ask God for help. Usually when we make requests to God it is accompanied by begging or crying or something like that. But my request was not really like that. All I was doing was complaining to someone by the name of God, as if he was sitting in front of me. It seemed to me that he was answering that my situation was because of all the mistakes I had made in my past and this was the way I was to be punished. I was answering that this seemed wrong because it was not I who was being punished but my son. Why was my innocent son being punished for something that I might have done? I was asking and yelling at God to end this punishment because I was not just Ali, I was a father. Those problems should be *mine,* not my little son's.

I continued to berate God, asking him why. He is God and is able to do anything he wants and he is the one who made humans in his own image, so he must have had a plan for us to live our lives loving and caring for each other. But

that did not seem the way we were living at all. All we seemed
to care about was how to hurt others for no reason, like using
guns to go to other countries to take what we wanted, in the
name of democracy. This was not right and God knew that.
"This is not fair! Do something!" I screamed at God.

In that moment I was not aware of time and did not know
how long my conversation with God lasted. I was totally
unconscious of my surroundings and there was nobody else
there. Suddenly my radio came on with Bill's voice asking me
if I was ready for a pickup. I was forced back into reality and
I left that conversation with God to continue with my job.

Two days later, when I was watching television, I came
upon Oprah's show and the first thing I heard from her was a
kind voice coming from a warm and friendly face which said,
"You are not alone. I am here. I am your friend." While she
was saying that to millions of people watching her program
that day, it seemed as if she was saying it just to me. I don't
know why those words went so deeply inside me and became
such a source of hope but that's exactly what I felt. Her words
provided a lot of energy for me to deal with a situation that was
the major concern in my life. From that day Oprah became
my best friend who always brought me hope and gave me a
reason to try to fight with my negative feelings. She became
my third source of energy, after my son Pourya and my dog
Roscoe. She helped me get all the answers to my questions.
Nobody could change my mind about the reliability of the
source of those answers. Even when I heard other people say
negative things about Oprah, to me she was perfect.

Shortly after that night I began to follow her show whenever I could. Once on her show I saw a guest by the name of
Panache Desai who gave me an answer to my recent question
about punishment. He made me see that problems are not
punishment; problems are opportunities to learn from and
they should not drain energy in your life. You should be thankful for difficulties because later, when you look back, you will
find that those difficulties were the reason for your success.

The only success I was looking for was seeing my son

speak and lead an independent life. This time when I was ready to ask God about my confusion of whether to laugh or cry, I already knew the answer was that I should laugh and be happy with my life while I am waiting. I just need to keep trying and trying to get to where I want to be.

VISIT WITH OPRAH

In 2004 we finally were able to buy a house. We were excited to move to the new home as it was in a beautiful area with nice neighbors. We were very happy at our success at this moment in our lives. As we met the neighbors, we found that a lot of them were different nationalities from many different countries and we got along with some of them very well. We met a black lady by the name of Tina who introduced herself as a psychologist. She and I met at the park near our house where we walked with our dogs. After a couple of meetings we became comfortable talking to each other about our lives and asking each other questions and sharing stories. I happened to mention to Tina my desire to meet Oprah one day. She answered that she had seen Oprah three times so far and that she would try to take me to see Oprah the next time she came to San Francisco, as she did from time to time. I was very excited at the prospect of meeting Oprah and I waited impatiently for this to happen. One day I saw Tina who had a big smile for me and she gave me the wonderful news that I should prepare myself to see Oprah the coming Sunday night. Tina would be taking me. I didn't know what to say. I was like a kid who got his most desired wish. I grabbed her and gave her a big hug and asked her what time I should pick her up and how, when and where would we go?

I brought this wonderful news to my wife and waited for Sunday. At the appointed time I picked her up, dressed in my best suit with my car freshly cleaned, ready to drive to San Francisco to meet my hero.

The place we were to see Oprah was a big theater building in San Francisco. A lot of people were there, wearing evening clothes, walking inside the theater, appearing to have the same plan I had of "visiting Oprah." We found our seats and while we were waiting for Oprah to appear, I asked Tina if I could actually talk to her or one of her directors in person. Tina said she thought so because she knew someone who could help with that.

I had even prepared scripts that I was ready to show Oprah for her show. If I could do that, I thought, many financial problems would be solved for my family.

After a few minutes of waiting, the lights went out and the curtains opened to reveal the stage and very soon actors and actresses came on the stage accompanied by loud music. The actors started screaming which made me suddenly realize that I had found myself at the *opera* and I wasn't going to be meeting Oprah that night.

"Hey Ali," I said to myself, "again your English has brought a misunderstanding." I was afraid to ask Tina what was going on. After about an hour or so of watching the acting and listening to the singing and not knowing why Tina was crying from time to time, I went to sleep. Suddenly I woke up to loud applause and whistling from the audience and I joined in. Tina, with her eyes red because of all the crying, asked me how I enjoyed it. She asked me if I wanted to talk to the director now.

After a few seconds of looking into her eyes, I said "No, it is not necessary. I got what I wanted."

"Did it help you with your story?" she asked.

Again, after a few moments of silence, looking into her eyes and not knowing exactly how to answer her, I said, "Oh, yes. Thanks for your help. Let's go."

From the moment we left the opera house until we got home she talked about how beautiful the story was and described various parts of the story. I tried to follow her, shaking my head and smiling, but I was deep in my own thoughts about what had just happened, asking myself how I had made this mistake and what the correct pronunciation of "Oprah" was.

After dropping Tina off at her home and before arriving at my own, I realized my problem was not over. It would begin again when I saw my wife who was waiting to ask me the result of meeting Oprah. But, I just kissed her and said, "Hi, honey. That was good, but because so many people had come to see her I didn't have a chance to meet her in person. I need to find another way. Let's go to bed. It's late."

LAS VEGAS VACATION

It was summertime and my wife asked me about taking a vacation. She wanted to go to Las Vegas and my daughter and I agreed that this was a good idea. I started searching on the internet to arrange a trip to Las Vegas. While I was searching, I found a good promotion and called the company to learn the details. A warm and friendly voice greeted me on the phone and told me about their offer of four days and three nights at one of the best hotels there for only $100. All I would have to do was attend a brief, one-hour meeting with my wife where we would watch a short advertising movie and speak to an agent for a few minutes. She said the agent would try to sell us something but all we had to do was listen, and at the end we could say no and we could then leave with no hassle and enjoy the rest of our vacation.

I was very surprised and I eagerly accepted the offer. I picked a date and brought this wonderful news to my family. This was proof of how smart and powerful the leader of their home was.

The time for our vacation came and we left our home in our car, happily driving to Las Vegas. Our drive was uneventful and we just drove, talked and sang together on our way. We were already enjoying our trip.

At lunchtime we decided to stop at a restaurant. After I parked the car and as we were entering the restaurant, we saw a little dachshund on a leash outside the door, sitting and waiting for his family. I was in a very good mood and because I thought it would entertain my daughter, I stopped in front of the dog and stared at him for a few moments. I turned my head left and right and started a conversation with him by barking a little at him. He started barking back at me, non-stop. My wife looked at me and said, "See, even that little dog has a problem as soon as he sees you. Imagine how difficult it is for me to handle you every day."

We laughed and went inside the restaurant. We were seated at a table with a good view of the dog, and he could see us as well. Every time he noticed me looking at him he started barking at me again. By the time we finished our lunch and left the restaurant the dog was gone.

After two more hours of driving we stopped at a gas station. As I was putting gas in the car I heard familiar barking sounds. I turned around to see where the sound was coming from and saw that same dog sitting in the adjacent car. He had recognized me and again started barking. I looked at my family who had also noticed the dog and what was happening and we all laughed again.

We drove on for a long time and finally we were in Las Vegas at our hotel. We walked into the lobby to check in. Unbelievably, I heard a familiar voice immediately. Our friend the little dog was in the same hotel and had noticed me among the hundreds of people and was again barking at me from the distance.

The next day, early in the morning, we woke up, ate our breakfast and my wife and I left our children in the room for our meeting. We had planned on being gone for only an hour and then we would all go and tour Las Vegas. The arrangements for the meeting were efficient and we were picked up by a shuttle and taken to our meeting place.

At the meeting we watched a fifteen-minute film and then we were assigned to an agent who invited us to sit at a table to talk. He was very friendly and introduced himself as Uncle Sam. He said that the reason he was called uncle was because he loved people and wanted everything to be good for the people he loved, including wonderful future vacations to help us enjoy our lives. He was a fifty-year old black man, dressed very nicely with a beautiful smile which displayed every one of his white teeth.

By this time I knew what was going on and I knew that to be successful today I had to just listen to him for a while, as I had agreed to do, and after a while I would just decline his offer without any excuse or explanation and leave the place. I was sure that my wife, since she didn't know English that well, would not be a problem.

When Uncle Sam finished explaining his offer he focused on my wife and said some very complimentary things about how nicely she was dressed and how intelligent she looked. I did not know how my wife understood what he was saying about her, but she was very pleased by everything he said and even added more that he had forgotten to say, through me, her translator.

Our one-hour meeting turned into a three-hour conversation between my wife and Uncle Sam. I was adding nothing to the conversation myself, only translating for my wife and Uncle Sam.

Finally, I ended the conversation by telling Uncle Sam that we really had to get back to the hotel as our children were waiting for us, and at that time we were not interested in accepting his offer, maybe on the next visit. We asked his permission to leave and were in the last group of people leaving the meeting. As we waited for our turn to take the shuttle back to our hotel, my wife turned to me and what she said made me think of asking God again whether I should laugh or cry. What she said was, "See, I told you to leave everything to me because I can handle these things much better than you."

We came back to our hotel to rejoin our children. Our daughter was furious that we had not returned for almost four hours. She angrily questioned us about our delay and before I could explain anything, my wife said simply, "Your dad..."

We left our hotel and started our tour of the many hotels in Las Vegas, enjoying the variety. We agreed with what we had always heard about Las Vegas being one of the most attractive places in the world. Everything was expensive there but to be honest, it seemed worth it and the people who built that city deserved to enjoy their high income. Every hotel was designed with a different theme to attract visitors. At the Venetian, my wife and daughter were as usual focused on the stores, shopping and looking at all the dresses, and my job was to pay for things and carry their bags while watching my small son, who was with me all the time.

There was a canal inside the shopping area with some boats carrying tourists in them, like they have in the real Venice. We decided it would be fun to take a little ride, and a break for me from carrying all the packages and holding on to my son. We were enjoying our tour and listening to the man who was piloting our boat singing Italian songs, when my daughter pointed to something on one of the bridges that we were preparing to float under. I looked to where she was pointing and saw that same little dog walk off the bridge to the railing and once again start barking at me. I don't know how he found me again, among all those people in that very crowded place, but he was very excited to show that he recognized me. "Oh my God," I thought. "Why? What did I do?" To make a story for my daughter, I said, "He knows your mom has some problem and he is not happy to see her."

My wife said, "No, he was wondering why a beautiful lady like me is walking with a man like you."

As usual, we laughed at our conversation and waved at the dog as we passed.

When we had finished visiting all the hotels that day, on our walk back to our hotel someone handed me an advertising card with a picture of a sexy girl on it with her name and phone number. I realized this must be an advertisement for prostitution. My wife saw the card and became upset and refused to talk to me for the rest of the night. My explanation was not acceptable to her and she was in a bad mood until the next day when our trip was over.

Overall, we were all very happy with our vacation and fortunately did not encounter that little dog again on our way home.

THE LAW

I was working at my courier job one evening, delivering mail, when I was pulled over by the police for stopping my car incorrectly at an intersection. There was a stop sign and my car stopped a little beyond the line instead of behind it. I told the officer that the reason I stopped past the line was because there was a tall fence that obstructed my view and I couldn't make sure all directions were clear. I told him this was not my fault and that the wall or the line in the street was the problem and should be fixed, but he gave me a ticket anyway and said he was not the judge and he was only doing his job enforcing the law.

"Law" is a word that implies safety and comfort to people since we left the caves and created a society to live in. Laws help control and protect our lives. We should accept and follow laws in order to have a good life and be happy. Laws are imposed on people to protect and control them but sometimes they can be wrong, such as in the case when I received that ticket. I did not agree that particular law was right and I decided to go to court to explain why I had done what I did.

During my trial, after the officer offered his explanation for why he had given me the ticket, I started to give my defense. I provided some pictures of the intersection carefully mounted on a board which I thought would clearly prove that this incident was not my fault and that the problem was with the wall and the placement of the lines. However, the judge decided to accept the explanation of the police officer and denied my defense. I lost the case but in my opinion the judge should have made his decision by checking to see if what I had said was true instead of simply supporting the police. A judgment should always be based on testimony and evidence. Judges should never make decisions based on feelings and subjectivity. I knew that judges always follow the book which was created by a group of people who made the laws. All the evidence I brought into the court was true and I thought he should really check out that place and then decide, but it did not happen that way.

I was very disappointed when I left the court and tried to determine what had been the problem in this case. Was it my English or was the problem with the law? I didn't know what I should do in this case. Should I ignore what happened or try to make myself more clear to the judge? I decided I should simply accept the decision because the judge was busy with a number of cases and he should support the police in the first place because they enforce the laws.

A few months later, I found myself in the position of the plaintiff instead of the defendant when I filed a suit against an attorney. I had made a contract with this attorney and he had failed to do the job we had agreed on. I had already paid him in full and he had refused to refund any of my money and tried to disappear. But this time I was in the place of the police, as the plaintiff.

When this attorney showed up in court as the defendant, he was wearing very poor and shabby clothing and appeared with an unshaven face looking more like a homeless person than an attorney. This surprised me because the previous times I had seen him as his client, he wore very nice suits and drove a nice Mercedes Benz. He should have appeared in court dressed much better out of respect for the court. I had taken care to honor the court by wearing my best suit (the same one I had worn to my first court appearance).

After I made my statements against the defendant and the judge heard his side, this time the judge made her decision in my favor and found him guilty and asked him to pay me back what he owed me. He said he didn't have any money and was broke. The judge told me the court could not do anything for me other than to find him guilty and agree that he should pay me back, but it could not collect for me. It would be up to me to find a way to get my money. At this point, we found that he had not been practicing law for a few years and what he had said to me earlier about being an attorney was a lie.

The judge advised me that I should keep my eyes open and be careful about finding the right people to help me the next time I wanted to hire someone. The law in this instance could not do anything against him and in the eyes of the law he had the same rights as I did.

Then she asked me to leave the court so she could call the next case. I left that day with a lot more questions in my mind. In this life, each of us has a job to do and the law is there to protect us against the wrongs done to us by others. The police control people by enforcing the law but why did this man, who said he was an attorney but was practicing law without permission, get away with no repercussion? The law should have imposed some kind of punishment on him. It should not be my job to do this.

I struggled with these two cases. In the first case, I had accepted the decision of the judge even though I felt it was wrong, and I had to pay a fine for what I had done. In the second case, even though I was right, I still didn't get any satisfaction since I was left with no compensation and would have to collect on my own.

People support the law and the government by paying taxes and we should be comfortable in this country because of the law which is supposed to be there to protect us. The eyes of the law should be open to make sure people are not doing anything wrong. But this is not what happened and that day I found that I could not expect much protection and I needed to be my own "police." I had to be responsible to make sure nobody did anything wrong to me but if it did happen, I should not expect justice in the courts, which I had felt confident would happen. This is unfortunate because the right to justice is a big part of human civilization and it is an important reason why humans consider themselves the most important of God's creations. After the revolution in Iran the group that has taken power appears in the news frequently and is considered a group of people who use force to control people instead of building loyalty by appealing to their minds and hearts. This is what Iranian people suffer so they have come to expect the worst from their justice system. On the contrary, in the U.S. people have expectations of justice in their country which is also what I expected to find.

I left my country to provide a better future for my son, and to do that I had no other choice but to actually break Iranian law. Because I was retired from the Air Force as an officer with a high rank I did not have permission to become a citizen of the U.S. By doing that I broke Iranian law. As my punishment I lost my retirement salary and all the other benefits I had earned, as well as all my assets. Whether the reason I had done what I had done was excusable or not didn't matter. I had broken the law and by doing that I had agreed to the consequences. After ten years of being busy with my life in the U.S. I decided to visit my own home town. The day after I arrived in Iran I had to appear in court to explain the reason for breaking the law by leaving, and staying away for such a long period of time. After I explained my reasons the judge decided that my salary should be reinstated and my assets should be returned to me. Under my particular circumstances, leaving without permission was forgiven, regardless of what the law said. I was not surprised by this ending because I was raised with the idea that obeying the law should bring real justice to our lives. Because humans have hearts they can see that the reality is that all the words in the law books are only there to help us be secure in our lives. The fact is that our decisions should be based on the truth, only the truth.

The result of my second court appearance in the U.S. brought me understanding of the laws in the best country on earth. "Law" is just a word on paper that people use to say they are doing their job. It can be right or wrong, but the expected result can be something very different. As I sat in my car reviewing what had just happened, I asked myself what the problem was. Was it my English? It could not be that because I knew English very well...

PIZZA SHOP

I started to look for another part-time job in order to improve our financial situation. Because of my son I was not able to take a job that would require me to be away from home all day long. I needed to be available to care for him and work with him. I found a part-time job that allowed me to work at night at a pizza restaurant near my home. My job was to deliver pizza to homes and my income was minimum wage plus tips. The pizza shop was a busy and very popular restaurant in my area with around eighteen employees working all the time until midnight.

My ideas about pizza shops and the people who did this kind of work were based on my preconceived notions. Even though now I was one of them I did not think someone with my prestigious background belonged there. My expectation was to find my coworkers a group of uneducated and ignorant people. Shortly after starting my job, however, everything changed. As I met my coworkers and talked to them, I learned that most were from Afghanistan and they were mostly all very well educated. Some had been doctors. One was a specialist in heart surgery. Another had a master's degree in law and was the brother of one of the recent presidents of that country. These men had left their country because the leadership had brought their country to war and caused much suffering to their people. Because my coworkers had left Afghanistan with no documentation of their education they could not work in their real fields in this country, so to support their families they accepted work at this level.

After a couple of weeks of working for that restaurant and being in the company of my coworkers, my understanding and attitude about the different kinds of jobs and the people working in them changed. I could open my mind about the truth and feel better about the work I was doing to support my family. I was no longer judgmental about people I met in my life.

One night when I was delivering a pizza to a customer, I met an old lady around seventy years old who lived in a senior retirement community. She appeared at the door dressed nicely, with her face heavily made up and wearing lots of jewelry. She introduced herself as Mrs. Jones and she invited me inside to bring the pizza into the kitchen and be paid there. I accepted the invitation and entered her home. She lived in a small condo with what seemed like thousands of pictures on her walls and tables, competing for space with many little statues and vases filled with fake flowers. It was very clean but it was so crowded that there was very little room to walk around inside the house.

She asked me the price of the pizza and I told her it was $17.25. She asked me my name and followed with many questions about my family, their names and ages, etc., to know who I was. I didn't have any option to refuse the interview. The information about me, however, was not enough and she started telling me all about herself, her children and grandchildren, their names and ages, showing me their pictures as she named each one. After introducing me to her entire family through the pictures, the story was still not finished. She asked me to stay and try the cookies she had just baked. This was not a question, really; she ordered me to do it with no option to refuse.

I accepted her invitation and hoped she would finish her story. First she asked me to wash my hands. I responded with a smile and quickly washed my hands at the sink. I prepared to try one of her cookies and I realized she was expectantly waiting for my opinion. I said, "Mrs. Jones, it is delicious!"

My job was still not finished because there were seven different kinds of cookies and I had to try them all and give her my opinion on the taste of each. I tried each cookie and was still waiting to be paid for the pizza I had brought her so I could leave her to continue my job.

Her next statement surprised me because she told me she sells the cookies for $0.75 each and since I had eaten seven cookies, I owed her $5.25, which she deducted from the price of the pizza and so she gave me only $12.00 with another cookie as my tip. I really didn't know what to say, but finally I said with a satisfied smile, "Thank you, Mrs. Jones, for your business with us."

I left her home after spending over half an hour to go back to my restaurant to return to my job. I had lost $5.25 in cash and no tip. I was happy for Mrs. Jones that she had been clever enough to use my company to make herself a little bit busy that night and make a profit by selling me the cookies.

At the pizza delivery job many different situations came up. One time I was very sad when I delivered a small pizza to a family with a number of hungry kids and the parents were not able to pay, or the times I delivered a large pizza to only one or two persons and I knew that most of that pizza would probably be thrown away and wasted. Sometimes I delivered to people during happy times, such as parties, and occasionally I would be invited to join their party.

Many times I had some exciting moments of adventure. In the city where I delivered there was a private, gated golf course community called Castlewood, filled with large, expensive homes located among very tall and old trees. One night I was delivering pizza to one of these big homes. From the street, after passing through the gate, I drove down the private road about a hundred feet through the trees in the dark. I stopped my car by the house, grabbed my pizza and walked to the door. There really was not enough light outside and not even many lights inside. I pressed the old fashioned doorbell, which was in the shape of a skull. After almost a full minute, the door opened by an automatic door opener and a lady's voice could be heard through the intercom inviting me inside. As I entered I found myself in a large castle-like room with old-fashioned furniture and crystal chandeliers. A few dim lights were on in some parts of the house. In front

of me was a large winding staircase which could be entered
from two sides. As I was waiting for my customer to come,
I heard a very unfriendly voice by my side, which I quickly
discovered came from a German Shepherd who was watching me from behind, baring his white teeth. I was more than
a little frightened by this but I said very softly, "Hi, buddy,
it's OK, I just brought pizza," hoping this would be enough
to keep the dog from attacking me. I was still waiting for my
customer to come and after a few seconds I heard her voice
again asking me to bring the pizza to the room where she was
waiting for me. She gave me the good news that the dog's
name was Frankie and he wasn't going to hurt me as long as
I followed the rules.

Slowly and carefully I walked down the hallway to meet
my customer and I found her in a big room with a king-sized
bed in the center and a few dim, soft lights on in some of the
corners. My customer was an old lady with white hair and
a cane in her hand, sitting in a rocking chair, staring at me
without moving. First I waited for her to tell me my next step
but it seemed that I had to say something. "Hi ma'am," I said.
"Where would you like me to put this pizza?"

After a few seconds, while Frankie was still watching me
very intently to make sure I didn't make any wrong moves,
she pointed to a table with her cane, and I put the pizza on
the table as she had ordered. Then she asked me to go to the
kitchen and bring her a diet coke from the refrigerator with
a glass. I didn't have any choice, so I did what she asked
while Frankie followed me all the time and watched me to
make sure I didn't do anything wrong. As I was coming back
down the hallway, the big clock started chiming very loudly
to indicate that it was 12:00. I had a very ominous feeling
and began to walk more slowly, but Frankie encouraged me
to pick up my speed by his friendly voice. When I put the
soda and glass on the table next to the pizza, I again looked
at the old lady to find out what she wanted me to do next, or
if she was finished with me and I could get my money and
leave. At this point, whether she wanted to pay or not didn't

matter to me anymore with Frankie at my side. I just wanted to get out of that place.

She was staring vacantly at some point in the room, sitting in her chair with her cane in her hand, not paying any attention to me. After a few seconds, I called out, "Ma'am, ma'am, can I go now?" I received no response from her.

I gently approached her by a few steps, repeating my question and still getting no answer. For the third time, when I was very close to her, I bent slightly over her to see her face closely to ask again, suddenly she made me jump back with a small scream as she jerked her face up and focused her eyes on me and very loudly asked, "Don't you want your money?"

I looked at Frankie who seemed to be laughing at me this time and this made me feel that I was finally safe. I didn't know what to say. I blurted out, "Money, money? Yes, yes, yes, no, yes, yes. If you want me to?" She pointed to her desk, which was in the far corner of the room, and asked, "How much is it?" Quickly I said, "Twenty dollars if you don't mind—and if you do, just pay me whatever you wish."

She said, "Take your $20 and take $10 for your tip. Is that enough?"

"Oh, yes, ma'am," I said.

After I took my money in the amount she had offered me, I looked at her face for permission to leave her home. It seemed Frankie knew his job because before I could say anything, he walked to me and guided me to the door and waited for me to close the door behind me.

I was startled by the call of an owl on my way to the car which made the whole event feel even more scary.

I turned back to look at the house and saw that Frankie was still watching me through the glass door, making sure I didn't make any false moves as I left that castle.

As soon as I entered my car, I immediately locked all the doors and made sure the windows were rolled all the way up. I drove away, never taking my eyes off the rear view mirror to make sure Frankie, or one of his friends, was not following me.

THE DINNER PARTY

Since we had come to the U.S. and had come to terms with the situation we were in with our son Pourya, we had given up any kind of socializing in other people's homes. We generally turned down invitations to parties because it was difficult going places with our son. He was not happy to sit and visit with people—he liked to walk around and touch everything he saw in a new environment. One of us always had to be with him to control his behavior and to make sure he didn't damage anything. This was particularly hard for my wife but I adapted myself to the situation since I believe a human has the ability to accept any changes in his life and modify himself to match whatever situation is presented.

One day we were invited to a dinner party by a friend I had known for many years. The only way I could convince my wife to accept the invitation was to agree that I would assume total responsibility for watching Pourya that evening, leaving her free to enjoy the party.

On the day of the party, after spending hours dressing in our best clothes and carefully leaving the house at exactly the time we were told the party would start and not a minute sooner, with still an hour to drive to get to our destination, we were on our way.

In our culture, how one dresses is very important. Even if we don't have enough money to buy food, we would never think of showing up to a party in anything but the best clothes we can acquire. It also often happens that people present themselves with the highest possible job and prestige and have no difficulty lying about their real occupation in these social situations. It is also considered very sophisticated to show up late to a party.

There were couples of several different nationalities cordially chatting with each other when we arrived. Shortly after our arrival, this peaceful conversation turned into a battlefield as the participants in the discussion each felt the need to prove that his or her opinion was the correct one. Because of my assigned task of staying with my son, I did not participate but I overheard one man insisting with scientific arguments that the sum of two plus two was really five and what we had understood since we were children was completely wrong. This pronouncement did not go over well with most of the ladies in the room and some of them began to argue that with men in power this was the kind of result to be expected. If women ran the world, they asserted, their wonderful gender would fix all the problems. Quickly the party turned into a war between women and men, each trying to convince the other that theirs was the superior sex.

I was not a participant in the conversation, as I was walking back and forth with my son between rooms, and the only other person not enthusiastically involved was a man I found out later was gay. Women were blaming problems on the pride men feel in possessing a penis. "Because they have one," they said, "they think they have power. To prove it, just look at the way they pee... Men very proudly and easily do it anywhere. They like to show their superiority by the strength and quantity of the flow, and their ability to write or draw something with their stream. They feel superior because women cannot do this. But women can control men by leaving a button or two undone on their blouses, or obtaining breast implants, or wearing very short skirts. This will make any man give up temporary control of a situation."

This conversation continued until the end of the party. When we left the party, there was still no resolution to this discussion.

I had been introduced at the party as someone I was not, someone with a very important job, which I did not have. I left the party at the end without having even once been asked for my card by any of the other wealthy business owners, doctors, lawyers and executives in attendance, or being offered one of theirs. Since I knew my story was a lie, I wondered if all of them had presented fake identities as well.

When we went to bed that night, I couldn't go to sleep. I was thinking about what had happened and whether I would have behaved differently and participated in the discussion the same way as the others if I didn't have Pourya with me. I thought about power and what it really was. Was power a positive or negative thing for people to have? Did it make them happy or did it destroy happiness in their lives? The problem for us is that we never pay attention to history, which could bring the answers to our questions. For example, if we look at the history of the U.S. we can see many examples of what people have done with power—both right and wrong applications of it. For example, at the time Bill Clinton was president, people were enjoying the best financial situation in their history and were not involved in any wars. Clinton showed the value of his power as president. When President Obama started his term as president his hair was still all black and he had no facial wrinkles. The country was suffering through wars in many places and the economy was one of the worst it had been in the history of the U.S. He used his power to change the situation even with all the obstacles he faced and to bring back smiles to the faces of people (but now his hair is gray and he has wrinkles on his face).

Power is a tool for people to use and how people use power is what is important. What power is and where it comes from can be irrelevant.

A few days after the party I stopped my car in the middle of the day during my job delivering mail. I wanted to take a break and enjoy my coffee. I had stopped at the top of a hill and I saw a group of boys around eight or nine years old playing together at the bottom. One of the boys stopped his play and went to a tree to take a pee. As he stood at the tree, some of the others started teasing him and in retaliation, he turned towards them and continued his job, spraying towards the boys. Some of the others joined him by doing the same and a "victor" emerged. The one who was able to produce the most pee raised his hands in triumph after he was done peeing longer than the others. This reminded me of the party and the topic of the conversation that night about power and how it affects our lives. To answer whether we should laugh or cry is based on who has power and whether he is able to use it in the right place for the right reasons.

The Egg-Breaking Machine

For a while I had begun to feel discouraged with my situation. We had expected to build our lives by working hard and saving money for a comfortable retirement, but after moving to this country I had to start over. I worked very hard every day for my family just to survive, and had no savings or investments for the future. I was very worried about this and started thinking about what I should do and how I could change the situation.

As usual, I brought my question to my lovely friend Oprah, and on one of her shows I saw a 64-year-old woman named Diana Nyad who swam for fifty-three hours in the ocean from Cuba to the United States. I was very inspired by this person with so much determination and patience, a warrior who never gave up and succeeded in solving her problems by believing in who she was and what life meant to her and always believing that victory will come if only you try.

She was right because life will always give us problems. They are part of human life. Problems are born with us and the only job we have is to fight for what we want as long as we are alive. We cannot change our age and that is not a reason to prevent us from handling our responsibilities. She gave me energy and the patience to try to make a better situation in my life.

One afternoon around Christmastime I left home to buy some milk at the store. While I was driving I stopped to help an old lady with a flat tire who was standing outside her car and gesturing for help from the other cars passing on the road.

I tried to change her tire but was not able to do it because she didn't have a jack and the jack I had was not the right type for her car. I offered to drive her to her home and she accepted my offer, asking me to help her move all the packages that she had purchased from her car to mine. So I did. She gave me an address and the directions to the house. While we were driving she told me that she had two sons and a daughter and a couple of grandchildren who were waiting for their Christmas gifts and she had been on her way to deliver them. After about twenty minutes I stopped at the address she gave me. She grabbed one of the packages from the back seat and asked me to wait there for her to drop it at one of her sons' homes. She came back shortly with exciting news... about the next house. At that moment I made the wonderful realization that I was going to be delivering packages to many different addresses and the most exciting thing was that there were more than ten boxes, which meant more than ten addresses. It seemed I had no other choice, so I said, "OK, let's go."

One of the packages was for one of her old friends and when we arrived at that address she asked me to wait in my car for thirty minutes because she couldn't just go in and drop off a package. This was a friend and she would need to have a cup of tea and a little chat with her before she could leave.

This process continued and it was five hours later before we were finished. She gave me a small box of chocolates and a warm smile when we arrived at the last address, her home, to thank me for the favor I had done for her.

When I finally made it back to my house with the gallon of milk I had left home for originally, I had been gone for six hours.

I was happy and feeling good for what I had done to help that lady and was feeling like I deserved a prize from my wife when I explained the reason I was so late. When I started to explain what had happened, that I had given a ride to a lady with a flat tire, before I could even start my story, I was attacked with non-stop complaining and screaming. I was accused of cheating by my wife, who didn't understand why she was always cleaning, cooking and raising my children and now I was going with another woman. In the end, I spent the night on the couch as I had no chance to explain what I had done. That night I couldn't sleep for hours. I didn't know the answer to what I had done or what I should do. Should I laugh or cry?

In my life I have seen many people get in trouble for mistakes that they either did or didn't do and get punished without having the chance to explain what really happened or give an explanation for what they did. The kind of reaction that they get usually causes more mistakes when they are not allowed to explain.

I think that most of the people who are living their lives behind bars may be part of the unfortunate number of people who were left alone and punished for what they did without ever having a chance to explain their reason.

Sometimes what they did may have even been a kind of revenge against those who took away their chance to show who they were and how they could be supportive to others. They were not given the chance to demonstrate their value as human beings who carried love for others in their hearts. That chance was taken away from them, bringing only more mistakes and pain and damage to relationships.

For a couple of days I was wondering what *should* someone do when they see an old person with a flat tire who cannot get help from anybody else? Apparently I had not done the right thing.

Following this event that gave me a lot of chances to think, I thought of a system that could assist anyone to change a tire quickly and with very little physical effort, no matter what their physical condition. I completed the plans for my invention with a diagram and built a prototype. I knew that with my invention anyone could change a tire very safely in less than two minutes. I knew safety was a major concern in the automobile industry and I made sure my invention was safe and easy to use. I thought it would be very useful for older people, those who have physical handicaps, and those for whom time is a critical part of their job, such as emergency vehicle drivers.

I was very happy and excited about my idea. I could create a very useful system for helping people and, in addition, it was a way to become rich. I had heard of so many people who had made millions for an idea that came to them in the middle of the night. I knew my idea was a great one and would appeal to the automobile industry, and I had the opportunity to bring it to the attention of best part of the world, the United States of America, The Land of Opportunity.

So I decided to try to market my invention. I discovered that I would have to obtain a patent for it in order to protect my idea. I took my invention to a company that helped inventors develop and market their ideas. When I walked inside the office building of the company I was greeted with a kindly smile by a man who made my day by saying, "Congratulations on your excellent idea!" He offered to provide assistance to make my invention successful for just a small fee of $1,500 for the process.

I accepted this offer by giving him a check for $1,500 and left him to his job while I took this exciting news to my wife. I told her we should consider ourselves rich already and to prepare to be able to get whatever we wanted or needed very soon.

Twenty days later, I received a phone call from my new friend at the invention assistance company, who asked me to meet him in his office as my book and my papers were ready. Those days I was spending a lot of time thinking about what I should do when I was rich. Should I quit my current job? Could I open a factory to build my invention so that I could create jobs for many people and also, the most important thing to me, afford to hire the best people to work with my son?

These were the thoughts I was having as I went to that company to meet my new favorite friends. When I walked into the office I was asked to wait in the reception area where I was offered complimentary coffee. I took the coffee and while I was drinking it and waiting for my appointment I started to speak with a white man in his sixties who said his name was Bob and was there with his son. The son had some strange looking device in his hands that appeared to be made mostly of wood.

After a few moments Bob asked me why I was there and I explained my invention in a very confident and proud manner. When I was finished, he told me, "You know, my friend, I don't want to disappoint you but these days people put value on ideas that can serve a large number of people at one time. Your idea is not able to do this, you know why?" Without waiting for my response he continued to explain, "One car usually carries one person so your idea will only be used by one person at a time. Plus, every driver knows that he should only use a car that has tires that are in good condition. Good tires never go flat. If they do, you can always call a company that will send some help to change your flat tire, so you don't need to do anything. In the end your invention will keep those people from doing their job and they will not be happy to support you with your idea and you will lose.

"So, I advise you, my friend, forget your idea and think of something better. Now, do you want to know the reason we are here? Come here. You are the first lucky person to hear our amazing news."

Again, without waiting for any response from me, he continued demonstrating his own invention. Proudly and excitedly he announced, "This is an egg-breaking machine! It was made by my wonderful and smart young son to bring happiness and a comfortable life to the people of this world. Everyone will be so grateful for what he has built."

He stopped and looked into my eyes for a reaction. I was silent while I was listening to him. After a few seconds he continued to explain how this wonderful machine worked. Ten eggs could be stored in the top compartment, which would automatically line up, and all you would have to do is pull up and down on the lever to break your eggs right into the pan. "You can decide how many eggs you need and break the exact number without touching the eggs with your hands. It is very easy to use." He continued, "This is so easy to use, anyone can operate this machine, old people, young people, anyone with a physical problem. Nationality or language is no barrier to the successful use of this wonderful invention."

Again he waited expectantly for me to say something. After a few more seconds, all I could say was, "Wow."

This was enough to encourage him to continue, which he did by saying, "You know, my friend, breakfast is the most important meal of your day, providing the energy you need to start your day. So, in the morning, when you and your family are in a rush to go out to your work or your children to go to school, it can help you make your breakfast very quickly. Restaurant owners will love to use this machine, too, so that they can provide very fast service to their customers. They will use this machine to improve their business and everybody will be happy and thankful to the creator." And with this he put his arm around his son and continued to say, "My genius son." Then he looked at me and said, "Don't you agree?"

I didn't know what to say. I was just listening and watching his mouth from where so many words were pouring out. After a couple of seconds, I could only say again, "Wow."

He was finally finished with his lecture and we were waiting for our friend to come out. Finally, a happy couple with big smiles on their faces came to us and invited us together to their office as they each had the same job to do. They started by congratulating both of us for our wonderful and successful ideas. They gave us information about what we could each get from our inventions when they took them to market for us and how we would have a chance to be rich if we let them help us. All it would cost for their extensive and valuable services was $18,000 to market our inventions.

I was shocked by this offer and knew it was impossible for me to pay this fee as it was not what I had expected at all. I answered that I could not accept their help at that time and said that I would do it later when I could afford it. Before I finished declining their offer, Bob stopped me by advising me that I had made the right decision for my idea. "As I told you earlier," he said, "it will not be successful, my friend."

Then he looked at the couple and asked their opinion about the egg-breaking machine and whether they thought it would have a chance to be successful in the market.

"Oh, absolutely!" one responded. Then they both looked at me, this time without a smile on their faces.

So Bob accepted their offer by writing a check for their fee to produce his son's wonderful invention—the Fabulous Egg-Breaking Machine.

I realized I was no longer of any interest to these people and I decided to leave the place, asking permission to go. They nodded their heads, but this time there were no smiles on their faces.

I left that office with a broken heart. In the parking lot I stood for a few moments by my car thinking about what had just happened and what I was going to do with my idea now that the only chance for me to become rich at that moment was gone. I saw Bob and his son come out of the building smiling broadly, getting ready to celebrate their successful new invention.

At that moment, God brought me the answer to my question. I was excited again to recognize the value of my idea and felt that I should not give up and should continue to try my best to bring my idea to the market.

When Bob and his son reached their car, they found that their car had a flat tire and they needed to change it before they could leave.

I drove my car to them with a big smile and asked them if they needed my help. Without waiting for their answer, I left them with the job to do on their own: change their tire.

It has been several months since I have had my patented idea in my hand and have tried to bring it to the market. I have contacted several automobile factories and different people who might be able to help me with my idea, but I have had no positive result yet. No matter whether you have an egg-breaking machine or a new tire replacement system, you should accept the fact that it doesn't matter who you are or what you have, it only matters who you know.

SCHOOL FOR AIRCRAFT MECHANICS

Time was passing quickly and I was stuck with two low-paying jobs that did not make appropriate use of my skills and which, even combined, did not provide enough income to support my family or give me any confidence for the future. I knew I needed to try to find another job and decided to learn about options. I had frequently seen advertisements on television and received solicitations in the mail from various training schools and colleges regarding opportunities for fabulous jobs with potential for high income, prestige and a lifestyle to be envied. One day I decided to call one of them to get an idea about what I could do and what they had to offer. The phone was answered by a lovely and sexy voice introducing herself as Mrs. D. She persuaded me that the best idea was to come to the school and receive the details of their program in person. She promised I would learn all I needed to know to make a decision.

When I met with Mrs. D in her office, after receiving a complimentary cup of coffee, we began to discuss the various courses that the school had to offer. When she found out about my aviation background, she appeared very surprised and pleased. She said that although I had lost a lot of money and opportunities for wonderful positions from the time I had first come to the United States, it was not too late and I still had a chance to recover what I had lost by taking their Aircraft Technician course. With the knowledge that I already had and based on the current high demand for these skills in the country, I would have no trouble finding the perfect position in the area where I lived, ensuring the wonderful and secure future that I so richly deserved.

These words made me very happy and I was immediately disappointed in myself that I had wasted so much time and hadn't seen this opportunity earlier. I had to make up for lost time and make myself a more useful person for my family and for the people of the United States as well.

The problem was that I had been away from schools for many years and the idea of going back to school and sitting in a classroom with a group of young kids, in addition to the issues I already had with taking care of my family, was not so appealing. However, I realized that these were all excuses and obstacles that come up in life and if a man needs to do something to obtain the necessities of life, he has to just overcome the obstacles and do it. It is obstacles like these and how we overcome them that show us who we are. If we just decide what we need to do and can analyze the problem, we can come up with the best plan to accomplish our goals. Through a careful method like this, victory would surely be the result.

The first problem I thought I had, sitting in a classroom with a bunch of younger kids, was solved by Mrs. D who explained that these students were not "kids" but adults just like me. The second problem of how I would pay the fees was also solved right away when Mrs. D informed me that here in the U.S., people who want to improve themselves and contribute to their country were valued highly and there were many options for assistance through the acquisition of an educational loan with a very low interest rate which I wouldn't even have to start paying until I finished the course, and by then I would have a great job and the small payments would be no issue for me at all.

This news made me feel more comfortable and enthusiastic about starting the program, so I accepted Mrs. D's offer to sign up, all the while berating myself for not having done this much sooner and regretting the time I had wasted.

On the first day of school I entered the classroom occupied by about thirty men and women between the ages of twenty and thirty. Except for a few "foreigners," most of them were Americans. They were all seated in their chairs waiting for the teacher to arrive. When I walked into the classroom, I decided that in order to establish a friendly and peaceful relationship with the rest of the class, I should say hi to everyone. I did this and waited for their response. At first nobody said anything and there was just silence, but after a few moments they resumed talking among themselves, totally ignoring me. I thought that this rude behavior was either because I was so much older or because of my nationality. At that time, due to the misrepresentations of the media, Middle Eastern people had left a negative impression on American people.

I decided that regardless of their bad attitude, I had come here to learn. But I also felt the additional burden of having to show them that we could have a friendly relationship despite the political climate.

The teacher, an ordinary looking man around my own age, introduced himself as Mr. Burns as he entered the room. He gave each of us a form to complete, on which we were to write about our backgrounds. He explained this was his policy each time he started a new class so that he could get to know his students better. After we returned the forms to him, he reviewed them for a few minutes and when he finished, he looked at me and then informed me that he was very impressed with my background and he was happy to have me in his class and called me Mr. Ansari instead of using my first name. This show of respect initially pleased me until I saw the reaction of the other students, who seemed to wonder who I was and why I was in the class and especially why I was being addressed by my last name and whether I was a member of the CIA or something. Using my last name created a wall between me and the other students which made my job of trying to build a friendly relationship even harder. My experience, after many years of living in the world, told me that time and patience would fix the problem. The thing I should focus on was obtaining the knowledge I had come to this school for in the first place.

At this point I was still apprehensive but it was not my knowledge or my ability to learn the course material that I was concerned about, as I was familiar with many aspects of aircraft mechanics after my many years in my former career. I was worried about my English. Learning and using the English names for all the parts and machines and understanding English instruction kept me behind the others in the class. I knew I had to catch up if I wanted to finish the program and that it would take more work for me than the others. I had to carry an extra book, which was my Farsi/English dictionary, which I referred to frequently, as I was improving my English at the same time.

The first three courses were a little difficult due to the limitations of my English and having to refer frequently to my dictionary, but I was still able to pass the courses with at least minimum scores. Soon I was able to keep up with the rest of the class and it became easy to continue the entire program. English and learning new words were not so hard anymore and since I had to concentrate less on language I was able to observe conditions that were hidden from my attention before, such as the other students' attitudes and behavior.

Some of the behaviors that I found unusual were that the students kept their caps on all the time in the classroom, and that they would eat and drink during class. The worst was that they found the passing of gas in public to be a socially acceptable behavior and would even congratulate each other on the "quality" of their emissions. They seemed to take a great deal of pride in this as if it were a tremendous accomplishment to be able to produce the noisiest air pollutants.

The fact that they paid no attention to which restroom they used and felt equally comfortable using one whether it was marked for men or women, even though they may not have matched that label, was particularly bothersome to me.

One day during our lunch break when we had an hour and a half for lunch, some of the students asked me to join them for one of their favorite entertainments that had been planned over a week ago. I was quite curious about what this could be, but I didn't want to risk being denied joining them by asking them too much about it. I decided to just show interest and follow them wherever they were going. I followed them to a park near our school where there were already fifty or sixty students gathered.

They stood in a big circle and I saw one person with a guitar and another with a drum. I was happy to have been included and was looking forward to enjoying some music. I knew I didn't like the type of music these kids mostly listened to (Rap) but I could still pretend that I was enjoying myself and feel like I fit in with the rest of the school.

After everybody arrived, Eric, one of the students I recognized, entered the center of the circle. He began by welcoming me to the event in front of the group and said that I was a good friend to everyone and he asked the others to welcome me too, and they all said "Welcome, Ali!" I was very surprised by this and suddenly disappointed in myself that I had not recognized earlier that people liked me for who I was and that I was accepted as a buddy and one of them. I thought they had provided this party with music and entertainment for me. Eric continued his introduction to the event.

He said that in their tradition, newcomers were asked to start the ceremony by hitting one time on the drum. I gave the drum an enthusiastic thump and was completely shocked by what happened next. Immediately after the drum sounded, two guys came to the center of the circle and started fighting with each other. They punched at each other with bare fists for at least three minutes while everyone was watching and enjoying the entertainment. Everybody was enthusiastically and loudly encouraging their favorite guy to hit harder. Finally the fight was over and the result was two almost dead bodies bleeding from their crushed faces, lying on the ground.

Everybody left the show to return to school and while we were walking back some of the students looked satisfied with the result while others did not seem so happy. Everybody was asking me for my opinion. I was shocked at the entire event and didn't know what to say, but I tried to smile as I looked back at them and tried to remember how happy I was to have been invited.

School time for me wasn't that easy because of my schedule. In addition to going to school seven hours a day five days a week, I worked eight hours a day for six days a week in my full-time job and twenty-five hours a week in my part-time job.

This school was a new experience for me, one that I had never before had in my life. The teacher used pictures and graphs and movies and copies of parts of books as teaching material and spent a lot of effort just trying to make the class behave. A lot of time was wasted trying to get them to be quiet and pay attention to what he was trying to teach us. Since English is my second language, in order to help myself keep up with the speed of the class I needed to work harder than the others. I didn't have time to join them in wasting class time for fun. One day I decided to bring a small video tape recorder to record everything so that I could study after school hours, but the problem was that I had to spend a great deal of time editing and erasing unnecessary items like student jokes and comments which took up a lot of the tape.

After editing one tape I was surprised to discover that there was only ten percent useful information left on the tape and the remaining ninety percent was wasted. I still thought that it was a good strategy to help me learn but I decided to stop recording for a different reason. One day as I was preparing my camera the teacher announced that he had something to say to the class. "You guys are excellent students, smart and knowledgeable. I know each of you is able to pass every exam of course, but I can help you with these exams," he said. "I have a tape to help everyone learn better, but you have to keep it a secret between us and you cannot let anyone know outside of the class."

Then he played his tape which I discovered was a movie featuring Will Smith. Everybody was happy to watch this movie which was totally unrelated to our course. I decided to turn my own camera off and was thinking to myself, "What kind of help can I get for my exams by watching this movie? Is this the way students these days improve their knowledge and skills to provide for the needs of their country?"

I finished the course after one and a half challenging years. Despite the added difficulties for me because of my responsibilities, I was very happy that I was able to graduate with one of the highest scores in the class and was very proud to bring this wonderful news to my daughter. It was a lesson to her that people can get everything they need if they try their best and not waste time.

Now that I had received my certification, it was time to find the better job with the fabulous income that Mrs. D had promised me would be the ultimate outcome of taking this course. I applied at several places, one of which was NASA, who apparently needed people like me who were certified aircraft mechanics. Shortly after sending in the application, I received an invitation for an interview. I was confused about this because I thought my perfect background and experience and high scores in the program I had just completed would have been enough to be hired. Yet they still wanted an interview.

I showed up at the interview wearing my best suit and I was surprised to see four other students who had been my recent classmates there. I found out that NASA wanted to hire two people and I was happy that I would have someone I already knew working with me because naturally I was certain I would be one of the two chosen—but which of those others would be the second one?

After a short time a gentleman came to us with some forms in his hands which he passed out to each of us to complete. He said that these forms would help us provide information about who we were and our knowledge of the course material we had covered in school. There was space for a short biography about ourselves, then about thirty technical questions. They were quite easy to answer and I completed the form quickly.

One of my former classmates was a 29-year-old man named Gary who had served five years in the U.S. Air Force as an aircraft mechanic. This young man had already been divorced three times and was currently single. His body was covered with tattoos everywhere his skin was exposed and I assumed there were more where I could not see. He had earrings in his ears and his hair hung to his shoulders. As seemed to be the style at that time, he wore very baggy pants so low on his body that I was amazed that they stayed up at all. This was a man who never paid attention during class and was absent so much during our course that he really seemed to have learned nothing from the class. He asked everyone in the group for help with the answers to the technical questions on the form as he was unable to answer them himself.

In a short time, someone came back to the room to collect our forms and we were called into different rooms for interviews, which were conducted two at a time. I ended up being in the same interview with Gary. The interviewer, Mr. Jackson, was a large man wearing reading glasses who looked very serious and angry. First, he asked me if I had ever fought or talked against the U.S. when I was serving my time in the Iranian Air Force and whether I had any opinions about the terrorists who had attacked the U.S. I did not know why he was asking these kinds of questions for a job at NASA. He wasn't interested in my answers anyway because as soon as I started to answer a question, he would stop me in the middle of the answer with another unrelated question.

Some of these questions were about aircraft systems which I easily knew the answers to, but some of the questions were not even questions that we could be expected to know, such as what materials were used in the production of aircraft paint or how long it takes an aircraft tire to be manufactured in a factory from scratch. None of these topics were taught to us during the course of our training. Finally after about twenty minutes he finished with me after so many questions. The way he looked at me the whole time reminded me of the way my father-in-law had looked at me when I first asked permission to marry his daughter.

Next, he started to question Gary and this time everything was totally different. Gary was asked simple questions while he was gazed upon fondly by our interviewer. His questions were very easy and so basic even my daughter could answer them, like what tool do you use to unscrew a bolt. Even though Gary's answer of "a screwdriver" instead of a wrench was completely wrong, Mr. Jackson surprised me with his response of, "Wow! You are smart, my son," while staring at me with hostility in his eyes the whole time. Mr. Jackson continued by saying that we needed people like him at NASA.

Finally the interview was over and Mr. Jackson gave us permission to leave and told us that we would be notified of their decision by mail. Before leaving, Gary and I both went to the restroom. After putting some water on my face I entered a stall to do another job caused by the stress of the interview with Mr. Jackson. While I was seated on the toilet, wondering about what had just happened, I heard the door open and the footsteps of two men entering the restroom. They began a conversation and I immediately recognized the voice of Mr. Jackson who was telling the other man that he had just had an applicant who was presumptuous enough to think he could work for NASA.

"What kind of job?" the other man asked.

"I just helped prevent some kind of terrorist action," Mr. Jackson replied.

The other man asked why he thought that. Mr. Jackson continued saying, "This guy was trying to convince me to hire him, but I discovered his relationship to that ugly Bin Laden. They have the same eyes and the same nationality and almost the same name. So I made him very confused with my questions and I am going to reject his application."

After a few seconds of silence, the other guy said, "Oh, you are smart!" Then they left the bathroom while Mr. Jackson proudly replied, "You bet I am."

When I came out of the stall I looked into the mirror while I was washing my hands and then I looked at the picture of Osama Bin Laden on the page of the newspaper that was left on the counter by those two guys and tried to see any similarity between my face and his, but could see none. My name was nothing like his and we were not even the same nationality.

Oh my God, should I laugh or cry?

A New Chapter in My Life

After I received my work permit, I had a choice to make. My experience had come from my time in the Air Force and I could have found a job involving some aspect of flying. A job as a pilot could have provided everything I needed: money and travelling the world, in addition to the deep sense of enjoyment one gets from flying. Anyone who has flown an aircraft knows the tremendous exhilaration one experiences in the act of flying. This feeling is addictive and I loved it. But a job as a pilot, or any other demanding job, would have taken me away from my son for too long. I felt it was my responsibility to spend as much time as possible trying to help him learn what he needed for life and it would not be right to be away from him for extended periods. Childhood is short and my son was growing up so quickly.

I decided to go for my second choice of work in the U.S. and try to find a different kind of job that would allow us to survive, but also to spend as much time as possible with my son. This meant that I had to work either while my son was at school or after he went to bed at night. I did not gain a lot of satisfaction or pleasure from these kinds of jobs. My previous jobs and accumulated life skills had been targeted towards creating a comfortable retirement for my family. But my love for my son and my sense of responsibility towards him and his special situation was stronger than my desire to continue planning for my comfortable retirement.

My new way of living, working at nights, gave me a lot of time to study autism. I tried to learn as much as I could about exactly what autism is and what kinds of strategies or programs are available these days to help and teach autistic people to get what they need. I wanted to learn about what is missing for them and why they are this way.

Most of my free time was spent with my son at home, or outside when he was not in school. I spent a lot of time at his school as a volunteer to try to learn more about him and his problems and to try to learn some way to solve them. Spending time with Pourya and other autistic children made me understand that in general there is no difference between my son and "normal" children. I think children are a nation unto their own, representing true love which transcends all divisions created by adults, such as culture, language, race, religion, etc. I have learned that we should not have preconceived expectations from our relationship with children and we should not judge them. I felt very fortunate to be in the company of autistic children and I enjoyed the moments I spent with them.

After several years of being in this situation my experience and knowledge led me to the idea of opening a center for autistic children where they could get help from people other than family and school. The center would also help the families learn about their children's condition and receive emotional and practical support. I felt that I would be able to use the skills and experience I had accumulated over the years, doing a job that I enjoyed and providing a needed service. I hoped our facility would help fill in the missing pieces and help the children learn based on the techniques and skills I had been learning over time.

However, opening such an institute by myself was very difficult. Without money and the right people that were needed for getting approval, the project was practically impossible. But I decided I would do it anyway and the idea was never far from my mind as I searched for some way to make it a reality.

As God always provides for our needs, one day I happened to meet a woman in a coffee shop named Annette Musso. Our meeting was entirely accidental but when we started talking we discovered that we were in the exact same situation: She had an autistic son as well and we both had the same plan of opening a center for autistic children to offer respite care and to help and teach the children. Since this was such an auspicious encounter we decided to join forces and work together.

Over time we created a non-profit organization called Creative Autism Solutions Team, or CAST. We hoped to make all of our dreams for assisting autistic children come true and we were so happy when we could finally open our facility after all the difficulties we encountered along the way. It seemed that obstacles were placed in our way capriciously and organizations that should have been helping us build such a worthwhile and needed project were trying to stop us instead.

We spent a lot of time looking for a place to start our valuable mission and we foolishly expected that we would receive help from others in the form of financial donations or at least a reduced rent for a space. But these were just our expectations and not reality. We had to go with our own resources, which were quite limited. At least we had hope for the future and looked forward to the time our facility would be open and running.

However, we were surprised again and again by the requirements for permits from different departments in the city where we chose to open our facility. We had to have legal permission to open this kind of center and we had to overcome all sorts of issues such as safety and the permission of the community. We were dismayed as we were not opening a business that was planning to make a lot of money—we were opening a non-profit facility that was designed to *help* people.

Being forced to comply with one regulation after another before being able to open our center delayed so many innocent children from benefitting from our facility. These kids and their parents needed help *now* and we felt it was very unfair to have to attend so many meetings with the city who complained about sprinkler systems and other corrections which had to be made before we could get approved.

We tried to explain what we were doing, that our plan was so important and would do so much good. We explained that to be able to accomplish our goals we needed to focus our attention on our children and not on fixing sprinklers.

It should be their job to help us, not to delay us. This wasn't right. But this explanation didn't do any good and we got no help or any special consideration.

After the disaster of the whole application process, we finally opened our center and were very happy to finally be able to work with the children who needed our help. All of us who work there have been so gratified by the changes in behavior we see in many of the children we work with. We see results and improvements in each child and this is our reward. The best is to see the beautiful smiles on the faces of our children and their parents, who also have been very happy with the results we have facilitated.

Our sense of satisfactions is profound and from the bottom of our hearts we hope to continue our mission as long as we can and hope others will follow in our footsteps.

The Letter to Oprah

One morning when my family was out either at work or school I was preparing my breakfast as usual. At this time I was working at nights while my wife worked during the day so one of us could always be home with our son. My little dog Roscoe was sitting with me. He always sat and patiently listened to all the words coming out of my mouth.

"You know, Roscoe," I said, "since I found Oprah I have been trying to find a way to meet her in person, but to be honest I am afraid of meeting her. You know why? I love her for what she is and how she appears in my world. But if I met her in person... I don't know... Would she be the person I think she is? I have been wrong so many times because of my expectations and I am afraid that this time might be the same.

"I know I have changed and I am not that same person anymore with the wrong attitude about what my expectations should be, but in any case, I am human and it is very easy to make mistakes.

"I know I have fought with people who have said negative things about her and now I am talking the same way.

"Yes, you are right, she is still Oprah, our best friend and no matter what we might see, I would still love her for what she has brought to my life, and even if I see her drink coffee without cream and sugar, for instance, I promise I will still love her the same as before.

"You know, Roscoe, I am going to write a letter to her to tell her I want to meet her. Yes, I will do it right now.

"Yes, I know I have written her several times in the past and never actually mailed the letters. I know. I just said that earlier.

"This time I am serious.

"You don't believe me?

"OK, here you are, here is some paper and a pen. I am going to write to her right now and tell her my story and how much I want to meet her.

"What? My story is not over yet? I know. When I stop writing this time, I don't mean it is over or that I don't have more to say or that my pen is out of ink.

"No, of course not. But you know, Roscoe, every time I am free to write, Pourya is sitting on my right side and I have to turn the pages of his book and talk about what we see in the book which occupies my right hand, and you are sitting on my left side and I am petting you with my left hand and my eyes are on Oprah, watching her show. So tell me, how can I write? Life is made up of moments and each moment has a story to tell and pages to write, but in my situation how can I continue like that?

"You know, I am going to write her that the reason I want to meet her is that I want to tell the rest of my story in person.

"What do you think? Do you agree?

"What? You think I am kidding?

"Here you go."

Dear Oprah,

This is Ali and I am writing to you to see if we can find some time to see and talk to each other.

I have my dog Roscoe sitting with me and since my son Pourya is in school right now, I can write to you to introduce myself and tell you why I am writing you before I meet you.

Oprah, as both of us know, our lives are made up of so much beauty and we all have so many reasons to be happy and enjoy our lives. We have each other to help us overcome all the obstacles that appear as problems in our lives. This is because of the power of love, which came with us when we first entered the world, which is the energy that God gave to us to help us find our ways in life. In our journey through life the key is very simple. First, we need to find out who we are and then to try to get what we need. Finally, we have hope that we will receive exactly what we should so we are able to enjoy our lives and share our happiness with the people we care about.

But these days it is not easy to do this and most of us don't find our way because we are confused. It seems now that "love" is just a word for people to negotiate for what they want at that moment: money, a ring with a big diamond, sex, etc. But when they receive what they think they want, they will forget about love and try to use that tool at another time for another deal.

My friend, people don't seem to understand what real love means and what wonderful moments they are wasting by not knowing! This is sad. But why is this? What is the problem with people and why don't we all see things the same way? What can we do? How can we open our eyes?

I don't know about you, but what I found that was able to help me find my way in life was cinema!

Let me tell you how and why this was. People pay money to sit in a dark room to watch other people's stories. Is this just for entertainment? Of course this is one of the reasons, but not the only one. There are always lessons that come along with the stories told through cinema. These can help us find our own way home. But as we can see, people are still lost, walking in their own barren desert, confused and not knowing which way to go.

What I saw in the cinema was the story of human life in different situations. When we are sad or happy, when we are excited or bored, when we are experiencing a difficult situation, or when we are enjoying our moments and all of our problems have been solved (at least temporarily), we are the people who make the stories in the cinema: people with different characters who appear in the story of Life.

I have a memory of when I was a very small kid, four or five years old. I was the last child in a family with three sisters and a brother. Our family had the minimum income we needed to survive. My father was a strong, serious army man who lived in a very old-fashioned way, enjoying the power of being the leader of the family. The way he believed a man should act was to just give half of his income to his wife to run the household and spend the other half on himself. If there were any complaints from my mother or if she asked for more money for something, he would silence her immediately by yelling at her or hitting her. This would put an end to the complaint and he would continue his way of doing things.

My mother was a lovely woman who bore the responsibility of running our home and meeting all the needs of our family. She woke up much earlier than anyone else to prepare what we needed each day and she was the last person to go to bed at night. All she wanted was to do whatever she could that would bring smiles to the faces of her children. I don't remember ever hearing her ask for something for herself. Everything she did was for her kids. We were happy because we could always ask Mother for whatever we needed or wanted and she would try to get it for us. She was always there to support us in hard times, if we had problems in school or with our friends. She never said no to us and we were happy because we had her.

Oprah, let me tell you something about our culture. In Iran, if a girl wants to marry, her family has to provide all the furniture for her future home. We call this jahiziyeh. *Each time one of my sisters married, my mother would have to endure several beatings by my father for asking him for more money to be able to provide the* jahiziyeh *for that daughter.*

We were kids and we were not happy to see our parents fighting. We thought the cause of the fighting was my mother, because she was asking my father for money. We wanted her to stop starting a fight with my father because it was very unpleasant to see them fighting and to watch her being hit by my father.

One of those times, when my mother was preparing the jahiziyeh *for one of my sisters, something woke me up in the middle of the night. I found my mother sitting in the dark in a corner of the room, crying silently while everyone else was asleep.*

I sat at her feet and tried to comfort her by kissing her face and wiping away her tears. I asked her why she was crying. In those days, my mother didn't have any friends or relatives to talk to. She had only us, her children. For the first time, she began to share her problems with me, telling me about her needs and how my father never supported her and why she was not able to provide a good jahiziyeh *for my sister which was what she needed to start a new life.*

I was a very young kid at the time and I couldn't understand why one person was suffering because of another person's needs. Why should my sister have to have a jahiziyeh *when it was so hard for my mother to prepare it? Why was my father fighting with my mother instead of supporting her? Why and why and why?*

I had so many questions to ask and no answers came to my mind. All I remember of those days is that I worried about things that other kids my age did not. This brought me a new way of understanding. I saw myself different from others. But how was this? Was it right or wrong?

I didn't know; I was just a kid. But what was important to me in those days was that I should try to take care of my mother and I should help her however I could because she had talked to me as an equal, an older mature person. She was able to get some small relief from the pain she felt by sharing her problems with me. I told my mother not to cry and that I would get her what she wanted when I was old enough to have a job.

This made her stop crying and I was very happy to see her smile again. This promise made me feel my first strong sense of responsibility. That night had a tremendous impact on me and made me the person I am now.

Now let me tell you how and why I believe the cinema can help us find our way.

In those days life seemed so simple and everyone lived with the minimum required to sustain life. We had no privacy such as our own bedrooms, no television or phone—certainly nothing like the Internet. Going to the cinema once or twice a year was a big deal to us and plans to go were made far in advance and we looked forward to it with great anticipation. We enjoyed it so much!

After seeing a movie we would relive it over and over for several months, talking to our friends about the story we had seen, analyzing the characters, and discussing how a strong character in the film was able to overcome the evil of the bad characters. We discussed everything including what techniques were used for each scene.

As I said before, since that night with my mother I felt I was different from other kids and the way I looked at life had to be different from the way they experienced it. I felt that what was interesting for other kids in the movies should not be that interesting to me anymore, because I was different. I cared about my mother and I had promised I would support her in whatever way I could now, and more when I was old enough to have a job.

I felt I was responsible for what I had said and the promises I had made to my mother, while other kids did not seem to be burdened with these responsibilities. Because of this I knew I had to think and act differently. I felt that whatever exciting thing the other kids saw in the movies should not be that interesting to me and that I should look to find more meaning in them. But what was important? I was still a little kid and I was not able to find my answer. Whenever I tried to find my answer by asking the adults in my life I was told not to waste my time on these thoughts and to just go and focus on my homework. I had no other choice but to try to find answers by myself.

Oprah, life is all a challenge and we need to fight for whatever we need. Anytime we think of giving up we should realize that by quitting we would be leaving an important job in our life unfinished. At least this is the way I thought I should be in order to learn the lessons I needed to in my life.

My question about what parts of movies I should focus on and be interested in was with me for years. I had lots of different ideas but did not find a definite answer that satisfied me. The only thing I knew for sure was that I should not be concerned about the techniques of how people fought or killed each other. Those violent scenes were the most interesting to other kids but I was determined not to be interested in those things.

My first question in watching the stories that were told in movies had to do with how the same people, the actors, acted differently in different stories, showing different personalities. How did this work? Is it possible for a person to appear to be someone else? I am Ali, with my distinct personality. I behave a certain way because this is who I am. If I act differently, is it really me anymore? How could this be possible? I believed that the story I was watching was a true story and the people who were in it were real people with their own, true characters. That was what I expected, so how could they be different in another story?

If in movies people could change their personalities from one movie to another, were the people in my real life the same? Did their personalities change? God had brought us all to this life as equals but as we grow up we all change and adopt attitudes and personalities based on our experiences and our choices. We can choose to have a negative or a positive attitude. We can choose to love or hate, be jealous or have a big heart. All is a choice, but what we notice when we first meet someone is usually all positive and we usually don't see any negative parts. With time, we gradually see who they really are.

To me, the characters in the movies I saw were real and what I saw was that they showed exactly who they were with nothing concealed. But in my real life everything was different. I saw people act differently from who they really were, hiding their negative characteristics. But why? Was it wrong to show who they really were? Was there shame in being who they really are? They made choices in being who they were. While they knew what was right and wrong sometimes they still chose to do the wrong thing and would not try to change.

At first what I got from the stories in the movies was the ability to analyze people for who they really were and what they would accomplish or lose based on that. This discovery brought me the first answer to the question of what I should find interesting when watching movies. I also learned to pay attention to how successfully the movie makers brought their message to their viewers.

The other subject I focused on was to compare the problems in my real life with the problems I saw in the movies. In most movies there was a positive solution in the end—a victory. This was a valuable lesson for me, that I was not the only person with problems and that there could always be a victory at the end. When darkness falls at night, the next day will always bring light back into our lives. We just need to pass through the darkness of our difficult moments and focus on finding some light to help get us through the experience of darkness.

My dear Oprah, the movies I saw throughout my life made me focus on what really has value in our lives. We should be warriors and try to challenge the darkness and not give up easily when we don't get what we want right away. We should overlook the faults we see in the people we encounter during our journey and forgive them because they can't see the truth any more clearly than we can.

I also learned the lesson to always finish the task lying on the floor before me myself rather than look around for who is responsible for it.

The movies helped teach me who I should be as a husband with all the responsibilities that come with a marriage, and how to be a father to my children. My children gave me the opportunity to experience true love in my life and it is my responsibility to help them grow into the best persons they can be. As a father, I should try to take away all their sad moments, to shoulder all responsibility just to see them smile. I should try to be exactly who I should be.

I started to see going to the movies as my job, my duty to learn about life and to learn how to tell stories about life in the form of films. I believe it is the job of all artists to teach about the realities of life. Unfortunately I think now most movie makers are only concerned about making money. Creating art has to have a more important purpose than that.

I remember that after giving my word to my mother that I would support her, I decided to save my money for my mother and stopped spending on unnecessary things for myself, like toys or other things young boys want. I had a job now: to support my mother. I knew I had to put more effort into my schoolwork so that I would be able to get a good job to support her. I knew I had to just be happy with whatever she could give me and not ask her for more.

My goal was to become a film director. After finishing high school I successfully passed the qualifying exams to attend my chosen university. Although my dream all my life had been to become a film director I decided to join the military instead of going to the university. As a film student I would have had to pay tuition and not been able to make money. In the military academy I could instead make money right away and help my mother as I had promised. I was happy that I would finally be able to do this.

I convinced myself that the military was the best place for me at that time. I would be a warrior and because of that I would be able to make my way through all the difficulties in life. With that attitude I went through all the challenges in the military academy successfully and without complaint.

During the last portion of my education I was stationed in the United States. When I graduated and went back to my country I found big changes in Iran which were caused by the revolution. A revolution usually happens because people are suffering from a difficult life created by a leader, whoever that is—king, president, or emperor. We have seen this happen many times in history, in different parts of the world. Nobody revolts against the government if they are happy with it.

I had not grown up in a wealthy family and was used to times with very little money, but I never experienced the sufferings of poverty. I also did not observe terrible suffering in other people around me so I did not understand why there was a revolution. The way our Shah and the government had acted did not seem unexpected or unusual to me—it was normal and customary. It seemed to me that the majority of people were pretty happy and there was respect among the people. We are a nation with a very long history of civilization. We have an educated people and a very strong culture, with leaders like Cyrus the Great who embraced the values of human rights over 2,500 years ago and taught us not to judge people by the color of their skin or their religion. This should have given us understanding of what we were doing and how we should analyze what was happening and be able to solve any problems without revolting against the government. The revolution was not right, but in those days I was not looking for answers to those kinds of questions. I knew then and still believe that the future will clarify what people did and the reasons for their actions.

But I was a military man and my job was to support my government and protect my country and people from any enemies. What was making me sad and unhappy were the bad policies and actions that were taking place. For example, many wonderful commanders who were doing their job as officers, sacrificing their lives to protect their country, were executed. These were people I knew well and it broke my heart as we lost them. I wondered if this was the destiny of all honest warriors in the military who were just doing their jobs. I wondered why their lives were not given more value. The people in charge in those days were making some very bad decisions.

I knew history is a mirror of the truth of human life. I am sure that the full historical truth of this period will emerge sometime in our lives, hopefully in not too distant a future. I believe that the emergence of this truth slowly started with the beginning of the war with Iraq.

After the revolution an unnecessary war broke out between the two countries of Iran and Iraq. The reason for this war always bothered me. I didn't understand why innocent people should lose their lives for others who wanted to prove their power to each other. Power should bring life to people, not destroy it. Countries should be content with what they have rather than trying to steal from others who have something they want, and trying to take what doesn't belong to them.

I wonder why people pass through their lives making so many mistakes about who they are and what they are doing without looking at history and learning from it. Why can't they learn from the right people, like Abraham Lincoln, who believed that the value of people should not be determined by skin color? We should instead focus on who people are and what they believe.

But there was nothing I could do to stop the war, and because it was my duty all I could do was support my country and protect the people I loved and cared about.

Shortly after the war started the value of all those officers who were executed became obvious. With their leadership the war could have been over in a matter of weeks rather than taking so long, costing so many lives, displacing so many people, demolishing cities and damaging so much property, and destroying the beauty of our country.

I was getting older, though, and I started getting a lot of pressure from my mother to get married and have children. Obviously it would make her happy to be a grandmother. I knew marriage was the gateway to experiencing the power of love and I wanted to agree with my mother's *suggestion that I should marry. But because of my job and the war there was a strong possibility that I would lose my life during a mission, leaving my future wife alone and miserable. I felt that getting married was not a good decision for me at that time, but it was hard to say no to my mother. The only thing I could do during that time was make one excuse after another to justify a delay of my inevitable marriage.*

Let me tell you again a little more about my culture. The way a marriage is usually arranged is that the man will be assigned to visit a girl who has already been approved by his family, in particular by his mother. If he is interested in the girl he visits and she is interested in him, the deal is done and the couple will quickly proceed to marry. Usually the decision is made after no more than two or three visits, at which time the engagement becomes public. But even though I was trying very hard not to get married as long as my country was engaged in that unacceptable war, I could not refuse my mother's requests to meet various girls. I decided that the only way I could delay the marriage was to reject whoever I was assigned to visit, so each time I was able to solve my immediate problem and everybody would be happy. I remember having to visit more than thirty different girls, but I found some reason to reject each one. The excuses I used to reject them were not really true. Each of those girls had something that could bring happiness and love to a man. Love is not something we should look for in specific places or in people's faces. Love is not free. You have to pay for it by giving up a lot of what you want and what interests you, and focussing instead on what will make your loved ones happy. Love is giving, not getting, and it will happen if we know exactly what to expect and what we need to do to get it.

Finally, after a couple years of visiting various girls, it was my duty to make my mother happy and I could no longer delay my marriage. The last girl I visited became my wife and is my partner in life now. She gave me two wonderful children whom I love very much and who bring much joy to my life.

I don't know how it happened or why, as it was a normal visit like all the others and my intention when visiting her was the same as it had been all the other times, to reject her for some small reason. But this time I decided to say yes. After only a couple months we were married and started our life together. Prior to the actual wedding we enjoyed the moments we had together but during this time I was also distressed. I did not want to bring the burden of the jahiziyeh *to her family, which had caused so many problems for my family. I did not know if I could help the situation or not. I knew all I needed was her, not the furniture that she should bring to fulfill the expectations of our culture. I conveyed to her that I did not want her family to feel under stress for preparing a* jahiziyeh *for her. I reassured her that we could build a good life together on our own.*

    A few years later God gave us our two children, one after the other, and having them in our lives brought us much happiness. But the happiness left our lives when our son started the second year of his life and it was clear that he was acting strangely and not developing like other babies. After visiting a number of doctors and specialists we discovered his problem. He was diagnosed as an autistic child who would not be able to grow up like a normal child. We were told that he would need extensive assistance his entire life and there was nothing that could be done to fix the problem. We didn't want to accept this harsh sentence so for several years we continued to see other doctors and specialists and tried any program or ideas we heard about, hoping that something might magically help him. We were not able to get the help we wanted and we were just watching him grow bigger, passing days and months with no progress. It seemed like a very bad dream all the time. I was constantly worried about what would happen to him when my time on this earth was up and I would have to leave him. Who would take care of him the way that I do?

    When Pourya turned six years old and we had been unsuccessful finding any help for him we decided to try looking at what other countries had to offer.

    The circle of life is hard when we start out with not enough money or experience to handle our problems and needs, but as we pass through stages and grow older, time helps build our lives, step by step. With the energy we have in our youth we should be able to build a comfortable life, making it through the difficult times, and build a comfortable retirement for when we are older. We expect that by our retirement age our children will be old enough to handle their own lives.

    Moving to a new country meant starting a new life and forgetting about the comfortable retirement we had built for ourselves in our country.

    I knew this would be the price I had to pay, but my responsibility to my son and the situation he was in, and my dream of finding a way to create a future for him, one that he deserved to have, gave me the energy

I needed to leave my country, my home and extended family, to move and start over again.

So we came to the U.S.

Starting life in the new country, even with all the challenges and obstacles which we encountered, was not that hard for me because I knew that starting all over under any circumstances is difficult. My wife and I had already started a life together once and we could do it again. We were experienced!

Even though now I had children and less energy than when I was younger, dealing with the new language, culture and country could have been hard, but since the reason we were doing this was my love for my son Pourya, I got all the energy and inspiration I needed. We had a lot of hope in those days that something could be done for him. This brought light to the potential darkness of our lives. Living with an autistic boy of that age was not so common. Because of his situation and his behavior, it was very difficult to go out into public places like restaurants or movie theaters. Even hanging out with friends was not easy since we always had to watch him closely. When we did take him out in public there were always many people watching us. The way they looked at us was not very comfortable, but this was the situation we were in and we just had to be in public sometimes. We wanted to try to expose him to and teach him appropriate social behavior to prepare him for the time in his future when we would not be with him, so that he would not be alone. We could not complain or use his condition as an excuse to fail to do our responsibility to him. But doing so meant that we should adapt to his behavior and change our plans, giving up the things we had previously enjoyed doing, like going to our favorite places and visiting with friends.

This choice was particularly difficult for my wife but I was able to accept the limitations and solve the problem by going out less often. When we did go out I had to just ignore the eyes on us and simply focus on my son's pleasure in enjoying the moments. So his favorite things became mine and I was happy to make him happy. My wife was not able to join us that much so my world turned to the new situation of spending time with my son after my work. We tried to enjoy our relationship the times we were together, regardless of any obstacles. This life opened my heart to my son's wonderful new world. All the things that had seemed so beautiful to me had less meaning now and I became a new person. I was determined to enjoy the *life I had and to continue to look for answers to my questions about what it really means to be human.*

This time was different from previous times when my letters to Oprah were not mailed. This time I put the letter in an envelope and put a stamp on it and after we finished our breakfast, Roscoe and I went out and dropped the letter in the mailbox. After that, since it was a beautiful sunny day, we went for a walk and enjoyed that time together as we always did.

I felt happy for how much moving to the U.S. had changed me, after surviving the challenging problems which occurred because of the expectations I had created before life in this country. I thought how fortunate I was to have my three honest sources of comfort–Pourya, Roscoe and Oprah–to help me find the real meaning of life and truth, and the awareness of how the power of love can bring happiness to human life, if we open our eyes to see.

Thanks to God I finally had the answer to the question I had asked Him so many times.

I will laugh.

www.ingramcontent.com/pod-product-compliance
Lightning Source LLC
LaVergne TN
LVHW091309080426
835510LV00007B/430

* 9 7 8 1 9 4 0 1 2 1 0 4 8 *